Coordinating Distributed Objects

Coordinating Distributed Objects
An Actor-Based Approach to Synchronization

Svend Frølund

The MIT Press
Cambridge, Massachusetts
London, England

This book was set in Computer Modern by Omegatype Typography, Inc. and printed and bound in the United States of America.

Library of Congress Cataloging-in-Publication Data

Frølund Svend.
   Coordinating distributed objects : an actor-based approach to synchronization / Svend Frølund.
     p. cm.
   Includes bibliographical references and indexes.
   ISBN 0–262–06188–0 (hb : alk. paper)
    1. Electronic data processing—Distributed processing. 2. Object-oriented programming (Computer science)   I. Title.
   QA76.9.D5F76   1996
   005.2—dc20   96–24467
                                          CIP

To my parents, Agnethe and Rudolf

Contents

List of Figures

List of Tables

List of Examples

Foreword

It has been widely observed that software is in a perennial state of crisis. I believe that this crisis is in large measure due to the failure of research to focus on the problems of complex software systems. The cause of this failure lies in the historical roots of the theory of computing: programming has been defined in terms of the mathematical theory of functions. Functions inspired the concept of procedures, which provide both abstraction over a sequence of computational steps and reuse by parameterization.

As computation was used for more than numerical calculations, the need for more complex programming constructs arose. Quite early in the history of programming languages, Ole-Johan Dahl and Kristen Nygaard developed the concept of objects in the programming language Simula. By mimicking the real world in program structure, object-oriented programming simplified the task of doing simulations. The use of objects has since become very popular for programming in general.

Although parallelism is natural in real-world objects, concurrency in Simula was limited to coroutines. Carl Hewitt first proposed the concept of actors as a computational model for concurrent programming. The Actor model has evolved over the years and is now widely recognized as a way to unify objects and concurrency.

Although actors provide a general model for representing concurrency in distributed systems, the problem of actually building complex software systems has remained challenging: such systems not only have a large number of concurrent components, but these components can interact asynchronously to create an exponential number of possible outcomes. The need to coordinate the behavior of autonomous components to maintain coherence between components adds considerable complexity to the code. Such coordination involves dynamic temporal relations between events occurring in different components; it is usually implemented by explicitly programming a large number of messages and the responses to them.

Frølund's insightful observation is that coordination between components often involves temporal constraints between events at those components. Frølund describes a novel programming construct, called synchronizer, which allows an abstract, reusable specification over coordination constraints. Synchronizers provide a mechanism for reducing code sizes by an order of magnitude. Moreover, Frølund is able to demonstrate that such code reduction can be accomplished without sacrificing significant efficiency in execution.

What makes synchronizers particularly attractive is that they integrate well with currently understood ways of simplifying software construction: they maintain procedural abstraction, data encapsulation, and inherent concurrency. The net result is to raise the granularity of abstraction to a level that is much closer to the mental model of code developers.

This book should be read by both researchers and practitioners involved in programming distributed applications. To the researchers, the book provides insight into the problem of coordination that is central to distributed computing. To the practitioner, the book provides a programming methodology that is applicable to a broad spectrum of distributed software systems, such as process control, multimedia, and groupware.

In the end, software's perennial crisis will be solved only by revolutionizing how distributed applications are built and maintained. The concepts Frølund describes in this book represent a major advance towards that revolution.

Gul A. Agha

Acknowledgments

I thank my parents, Agnethe and Rudolf. Their patient support and encouragement made this work possible. I also thank my best friend, Brenda Kesler, for always being there for me and for putting up with my endless book writing.

This book is a modified and extended version of my doctoral dissertation. The work reported in this book was carried out at the Open Systems Laboratory, University of Illinois, Urbana-Champaign. The members of my doctoral committee—Gul Agha, Geneva Belford, Roy Campbell, Andrew Chien, and Simon Kaplan—provided me with invaluable feedback on my research. I especially thank Gul, my Ph.D. adviser, for his guidance and support, for encouraging me to submit my dissertation for publication, for writing the foreword to this book, and for extremely helpful and constructive feedback on drafts of this book.

I thank Carolyn Talcott for her thorough and very insightful feedback on drafts of this book. I also wish to acknowledge the very detailed feedback from Pankaj Garg, Reed Letsinger, Allan Shepherd, Daniel Sturman, and the anonymous reviewers appointed by MIT Press.

I have benefited greatly from countless discussions with past and present members of the Open Systems Laboratory at the University of Illinois. The laboratory members include Christian Callsen, Christopher Houck, WooYoung Kim, Rajendra Panwar, Anna Patterson, Shangping Ren, Daniel Sturman, and Nalini Venkatasubramanian. I especially thank Daniel Sturman for helping me to use the BROADWAY library as the basis of my implementation. I thank Shingo Fukui and Takuo Watanabe for the discussions we had during their visit to the Open Systems Laboratory. During my stay in Illinois, Ole Agesen, Rune Dahl, and Nayeem Islam all provided great inspiration and constructive criticism of my Ph.D. work.

Hewlett-Packard Company supported me in writing this book. I especially thank the members of the Application Engineering Department and the Performance Management and Design Department at the Hewlett-Packard Laboratories for their support in this undertaking.

The adviser of my *Candidatus Scientiarum* thesis at Århus University in Denmark, Ole Lehrmann Madsen, has been a constant source of motivation and support throughout my Ph.D. work in Illinois.

The College of Natural Science at Århus University made this work possible by awarding me a research fellowship (*kandidatstipendium*).

The Danish Research Council (*forskerakademiet*) has also provided generous funding for my stay in Illinois.

The research conducted at the Open Systems Laboratory was supported by the Office of Naval Research (ONR contract number N00014-90-J-1899 and N00014-93-1-0273), Digital Equipment Corporation, NEC, Hitachi, and joint support from the Advanced Research Projects Agency and the National Science Foundation (NSF CCR 90-07195).

Coordinating Distributed Objects

1 Introduction

The computing industry is moving from centralized mainframe applications to distributed applications that run on a network of computers. This transition is due to several factors. First, distributed computing offers scalability; performance can be maintained in the presence of increased workload by adding more resources to the application. Second, many applications exhibit physical distribution as an inherent property. For example, an application that connects automatic teller machines with a bank database is distributed because the tellers are distributed. In such applications, distribution is not a feature but an inherent property.

Distributed computing introduces issues that are absent in a centralized application. Different components of a distributed application may execute on different computers without a common clock and are thus inherently asynchronous. Moreover, the communication between different components of a distributed application may be mediated by a computer network and may therefore be subject to network delays. The network delays may be unpredictable since the network may be shared with other applications.

Asynchronous execution and arbitrary communication delays give rise to nondeterminism; that is, the relative order in which events occur may be different for different executions of a distributed application. However, many applications contain events that must always occur in a particular order. It is therefore necessary to coordinate the different asynchronous components of a distributed application in order to guarantee that events occur in a correct order.

Issues such as coordination make the construction of distributed applications more complex than the construction of centralized applications. It therefore is essential that distributed programming languages help programmers deal with the added complexity. To address this need, I introduce language constructs that allow programmers to implement coordination using high-level abstractions. I do not introduce a complete programming language but only constructs that support coordination. My goal is to provide general insights about coordination, and my constructs are not tied to any specific host language.

1.1   Object-Oriented Programming

Object-oriented programming is becoming the paradigm of choice for conquering the complexity of distributed applications. My language constructs describe coordination in an object-oriented setting; this section introduces the most important aspects of object-oriented programming. The basic concepts of object-oriented programming were first introduced as part of the Simula [DMN68] programming language. I assume that readers are already familiar with these basic concepts and thus provide only a brief summary. (For a more in-depth tutorial of object-oriented concepts, consult [MPN93] or [Mey85].)

Object-oriented programming provides a natural way to decompose a large, complex system into semiautonomous, encapsulated entities called *objects*. Each object has a state and a number of procedures, called *methods*, to manipulate this state. The state of an object is encapsulated; it can be manipulated only through the object's methods, not directly. The methods of an object constitute its *interface* to other objects. Objects interact by invoking each other's methods.

Besides encapsulation and data abstraction, object-oriented programming also provides concepts that help express the structure of programs. *Inheritance* is one of the more prominent structuring concepts in object-oriented programming. A *class* describes the behavior of a set of objects, namely, the objects that are *instantiated* from the class. Inheritance can be used to organize class descriptions hierarchically so that one class, called a *subclass*, is specified as a refinement of another class, called a *superclass*. Inheritance allows common behavior to be factored out and thereby reused. A superclass describes common behavior, and subclasses reuse this common behavior.

As an example of inheritance, assume that we want to describe the behavior of different kinds of vehicles, such as cars, trucks, and buses. We want to define a number of classes that each captures the behavior of a specific kind of vehicle. Inheritance allows us to define a superclass called `Vehicle` that captures the general behavior of vehicles—the behavior that is common to all kinds of vehicles. We can then define the `Car`, `Truck`, and `Bus` classes as subclasses of `Vehicle`. The advantage of using inheritance is that the `Car` class captures only the behavior specific to cars; the vehicle behavior of cars is specified in the `Vehicle` class. Similarly, the vehicle behavior of trucks and buses is also specified in the

`Vehicle` class. With inheritance, we have to specify the generic vehicle behavior only once. Inheritance also allows us to reflect the inherent structure of the application domain: we can reflect the fact that cars, buses, and trucks are all special kinds of vehicles.

1.2 Actors

I use the Actor model [Hew77, Agh86] as the underlying framework for distributed, object-oriented programming. In the Actor model, a distributed application consists of a collection of asynchronous objects that execute concurrently.

Objects invoke each other's methods, and thereby communicate, by sending messages. Message passing is the only means of interobject communication; there is no notion of shared memory between objects. Messages are asynchronous, which means that sending a message is a nonblocking operation. Messages are guaranteed to reach their destination eventually, but may be subject to arbitrary communication delays. Message ordering is not guaranteed; messages may not arrive in the order that they were sent. A message invokes a method in its destination object; we say that messages are *dispatched* into method invocations. Objects are reactive entities that execute their methods only in response to messages.

Each object has its own thread of control, which is used to execute methods in response to messages. Since an object only has one thread of control, at most one method can be executed at a time by an object. There is no concurrency *within* an object, only interobject concurrency.[1] Because an object can only execute one method at a time, each object has an input queue in which incoming messages are stored until they can be dispatched.

---

1. The Actor model as described in [Agh86] contains a notion of internal concurrency where multiple "reader" methods and one "writer" method can execute concurrently within an object. However, the semantics of the model guarantees serializability; the effect of internal concurrency is equivalent to executing the methods one at a time. I have therefore chosen to ignore the Actor model's notion of internal concurrency.

1.3 Coordination

Because objects execute asynchronously and because messages are subject to arbitrary communication delays, the relative order in which messages arrive at an object is, in general, nondeterministic. It is often the case, however, that an object must dispatch its messages in a particular order. For example, put and get messages sent to a one-element buffer must be dispatched in strict alternation; the buffer cannot consecutively dispatch two put messages.

Ensuring that messages are dispatched in a correct order is a fundamental aspect of coordination in distributed applications.[2] To address this need, I introduce high-level language constructs for describing and enforcing message-ordering constraints, along with specific applications in which message-ordering constraints are inherent.

Consider a distributed application in which n producer objects generate data for m consumer objects. A given consumer object can consume data from any producer object. Producers and consumers communicate through a shared buffer object; producers store data in the buffer, and consumers extract data from the buffer. The communication between producers and consumers is illustrated in figure 1.1.

We assume that the buffer has a limited capacity and can hold no more than MAX data elements at any point in time. With this assumption the buffer is subject to the following integrity requirements:

- The put method may not be invoked when the buffer is full.
- The get method may not be invoked when the buffer is empty.

These integrity requirements must be satisfied for the buffer to function correctly. The requirements give rise to a message-ordering constraint for put and get messages: the number of dispatched put messages minus the number of dispatched get messages must always be less than or equal to MAX and greater than or equal to 0.

One way to guarantee satisfaction of the buffer's integrity requirements is to arrange for put and get messages to arrive at the buffer always in an order that is consistent with the buffer's message-ordering

---

2. I use the term *coordination* instead of *synchronization* because it is a more precise description of the phenomenon of ordered message dispatch and because my constructs have a broader scope than traditional synchronization mechanisms such as semaphores and monitors.

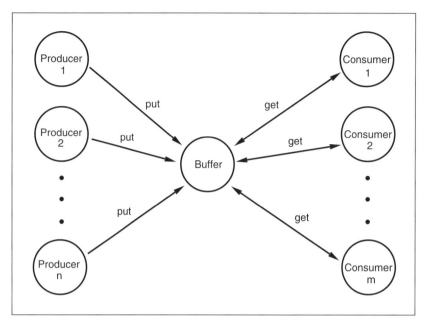

Figure 1.1
Producers, consumers, and a shared buffer

constraint. However, since the arrival order of messages is non-deterministic, arranging for **put** and **get** messages to arrive in a correct order requires that producers and consumers exchange "control communication" with the buffer. For example, the control communication needs to ensure that at most one producer sends a **put** message when the buffer holds MAX − 1 elements. The control communication would complicate the description of all the involved objects. Moreover, the control communication would include the producers and consumers in the implementation of the buffer's message-ordering constraints. Since the implementation of the buffer's message-ordering constraints would then be scattered across multiple objects, the buffer's encapsulation and modularity would be violated; if we were to change the buffer's message-ordering constraints, we would have to change the behavior of producers and consumers.

Rather than rely on producers and consumers to arrange for messages to arrive in a correct order, the buffer should be solely responsible for implementing its own message-ordering constraints. Rather than dispatch messages in their arrival order, the buffer should dispatch messages in an order that is consistent with its own message-ordering constraints. To implement such dispatch behavior requires that the programmer explicitly specify the buffer's message-ordering constraints and that the specification be executable; the specification should not only *capture* message-ordering constraints but should also *enforce* them. I define language constructs called *synchronization constraints* that allow programmers to write executable specifications of per-object message-ordering constraints.

Synchronization constraints delay the dispatch of messages so that the dispatch order is consistent with the message-ordering constraints. For example, if a `put` message arrives when the buffer is full, the synchronization constraints of the buffer delays this message until a `get` message has been dispatched.

Synchronization constraints express an object's message-ordering constraints as part of the object itself, not as part of the way in which the object is used. For example, the producers and consumers do not have to be concerned about the buffer's message-ordering constraints; they can rely on the buffer itself to dispatch messages in an order that is consistent with its message-ordering constraints. Since synchronization constraints express an object's message-ordering constraints as part of the object itself, they make it easier for programmers to express the logical structure of distributed applications directly. Moreover, synchronization constraints make it easier for programmers to maintain distributed applications since they can change an object's message-ordering constraints without modifying other objects.

The term *synchronization constraint* may be somewhat misleading since synchronization usually implies simultaneity: "Synchronize: occur at the same time; coincide in point in time; be contemporary or simultaneous" [Bro93]. Since synchronization constraints enforce ordered dispatch rather than simultaneous dispatch, they do not provide synchronization according to this definition. However, there is a long-standing tradition in computer science to interpret the term *synchronization* more broadly so that it is concerned with "correct order" rather than "same time." Rather than invent terminology, I have chosen to be consistent with the computer science literature and use *synchronization* in this broader sense.

The buffer illustrates a scenario where a single object, the shared

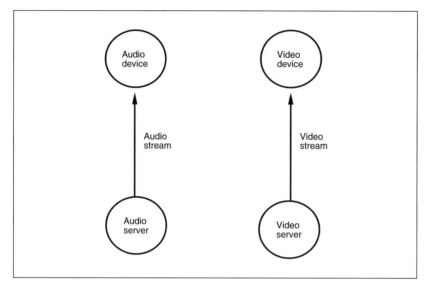

Figure 1.2
A distributed multimedia system

buffer, must dispatch messages in a particular order. However, many applications require that groups of objects dispatch messages in a particular order.

For example, consider the distributed multimedia system in figure 1.2. The multimedia system contains an audio device object that can emit sound and a video device object that can emit picture. Moreover, the multimedia system contains an audio server object and a video server object; each server generates a stream of messages for its device. Each message contains digitized information. Messages sent to the video device contain digitized video frames, and messages sent to the audio device contain digitized sound samples. The devices convert this digital information to an analog signal and emit the signal.

Due to network delays and varying workload at the servers, the order in which messages arrive at the devices is nondeterministic. But there is a logical relation between sound samples and video frames: certain samples should be played when certain frames are displayed (this is called *lip-synching*). Maintaining the logical relation between sound samples and video frames is an integrity requirement for the multimedia system. The integrity requirement gives rise to a message-ordering constraint for `play` and `display` messages: if the logical relation between sound samples and video frames is one-to-one, the difference between the number of dispatched `play` and `display` messages must be within a certain tolerance.

Unlike synchronization constraints that coordinate the message dispatch of only single objects, the message-ordering constraint of the multimedia system is concerned with the collective behavior of a group of objects (the audio device and the video device). In order to specify the message-ordering constraint of the multimedia system, we need a construct that allows us to specify message-ordering constraints that span multiple objects.

Moreover, we want the specification of these group-level message-ordering constraints to be transparent to the individual group members. For example, we want to specify the multimedia message-ordering constraint in a manner that is transparent to the devices themselves. We do not want to use a construct similar to synchronization constraints and describe the constraint as part of the devices. Describing the constraint as part of the devices hard-wires the relationship between audio and video into the devices, and it prevents us from using the individual devices as part of different multimedia configurations or as stand-alone systems. In contrast, we want to specify the multimedia message-ordering constraint as a separate and distinct entity that is associated with the devices rather than part of the devices. Such separation allows us to reuse the same generic devices as part of many different multimedia configurations.

A *synchronizer* is a distinct entity that specifies the message-ordering constraints for a group of objects. A synchronizer transparently delays the dispatch of messages by a group of objects according to user-specified criteria. A synchronizer can transparently observe message dispatch by objects in the group, and these observations can influence the way in which message dispatch is delayed in the future. For example, the criteria for delaying audio messages may be specified in terms of the number of dispatched video messages.

The multimedia example illustrates the notion of an *object group*. The difference between an object group and a collection of independent objects is that group membership limits the autonomy of the group members. Synchronizers allow us to specify object groups that require coordination of the individual group members.

It is common for group members also to be meaningful as stand-alone objects. For example, this is the case in the multimedia example: both audio and video devices can be used in isolation. Because we want to use the same objects as group members and stand-alone objects, it is important that group-level coordination is specified as a part of the group's behavior rather than as part of the group members' behaviors. Synchronizers provide us with the needed modularity.

Although both synchronizers and synchronization constraints express message-ordering constraints, there are significant differences between the two concepts. Synchronizers specify constraints as part of the *context* of objects, whereas synchronization constraints specify constraints as part of the *implementation* of objects.

Synchronization constraints often depend on the state of the objects whose message dispatch they constrain. By specifying synchronization constraints within objects, we can describe this state dependence without violating encapsulation. By contrast, because synchronizers should be transparent to objects, they should be specified external to objects as distinct entities.

1.4 Overview

Chapter 2 presents language constructs that support the description of synchronization constraints. In contrast to traditional approaches, these constructs allow synchronization constraints to be specified separate from the methods of an object. Constraints and methods are two different design concerns composed to describe the behavior of an object: methods describe *how* an object responds to messages, and constraints describe *when* an object may respond to messages.

Language support for synchronizers is the topic of chapter 3. Our notion of synchronizer facilitates message-ordering constraints to be transparently enforced on a group of objects. A synchronizer depends only on object interfaces, not on the encapsulated state of objects. The resulting modularity facilitates reuse and maintains the existing abstraction boundaries of a system. Moreover, synchronizers are specified as distinct entities, which makes it possible to describe groupwide ordering constraints as an aspect of the group rather than as part of the objects in the group.

In order to make the language definition precise, chapter 4 provides
a formal definition of the semantics of synchronization constraints and
synchronizers. The semantic definition in chapter 4 assumes that readers
are familiar with the basic concepts of programming language semantics,
especially the lambda calculus. Readers who are primarily interested in
the motivation for, expressiveness of, and practicality of synchronization
constraints and synchronizers can safely skip chapter 4.

The semantics presented in chapter 4 is operational in the sense that
it defines an (abstract) interpreter for distributed object systems with
message-ordering constraints. A distributed object system is represented
by a mathematical entity called a *configuration*, and computation is represented by transitions between configurations. Message-ordering constraints are represented as conditions associated with transitions.

A distributed implementation of constraints is presented in chapter 5.
The implementation is complete in the sense that it realizes all the proposed language constructs. The implementation provides experimental
feedback about the developed constructs, and I outline the trade-offs
involved in implementing constraints.

Chapter 6 presents my conclusions, summarizes my most important
findings, and points out directions for future work in the area of coordination for distributed object systems.

2 Synchronization Constraints

An object's synchronization constraints maintain its integrity and ensure that its methods are invoked in a user-specified order. Synchronization constraints express an inherent property of objects, whether sequential or concurrent: certain messages cannot be dispatched in all situations. With sequential objects, such message-ordering constraints can be an implicit part of the way in which objects are used. With distributed objects, the message arrival order is nondeterministic, and it is not feasible to implement an object's message-ordering constraints as part of the way in which it is used. In a distributed setting, message-ordering constraints should be described explicitly so that objects can maintain their own integrity.

Here, I present language constructs that support the description of synchronization constraints in an object-oriented manner. The constructs are not tied to any specific host language. I provide general insights about synchronization constraints. At the same time, I believe that my constructs could be incorporated into most existing concurrent object-oriented languages with minimum modification.

I show how synchronization constraints can be inherited and give examples of applications in which constraint inheritance can be elegantly utilized. I demonstrate how inheritance of synchronization constraints can be achieved by simple yet powerful language constructs.

2.1 Design Considerations

A programming language should separate the specification of synchronization constraints from the specification of methods. Methods specify *how* an object responds to messages; synchronization constraints specify *when* an object may respond to messages. A programming language should reflect this logical distinction between different design concerns of a distributed object: a primary purpose of a programming language is to help the programmer directly express the inherent structure of the system under consideration.

Besides helping the programmer express the inherent structure of a system, separate specification of synchronization constraints and methods also simplifies reasoning and supports modularity. Separation makes it possible to reason about synchronization constraints and methods in isolation, thereby reducing complexity. Furthermore, separation gives modularity: with separation of synchronization constraints and methods, the language supports the programmer in changing one design concern without changing the other. For example, consider a bounded buffer object. The synchronization constraints for a bounded buffer are that the put method cannot be invoked when the buffer is full and that the get method cannot be invoked when the buffer is empty. Suppose we wish to change the implementation of the buffer from an array representation to a linked list representation. The synchronization constraints are identical for both implementations, but the put and get methods must be changed. With separation, the language provides explicit support for the programmer to change the methods *in isolation*; the programmer does not have to be concerned with inadvertently changing the synchronization constraints as a side effect of changing the methods.

Since we are interested in distributed, object-oriented programming languages, our language constructs should provide support for synchronization constraints in an object-oriented manner. Support for synchronization constraints should integrate, rather than interfere with, object-oriented language features. Achieving this integration is an active area of research. Especially challenging is the integration of synchronization constraints and inheritance. It is a testimony to this challenge that numerous object-based concurrent languages, such as ABCL [Yon90], POOL-T [Ame87], and Procol [vdBL91], do not support inheritance.

Language constructs that integrate inheritance and synchronization constraints should satisfy the following two criteria:

1. The correct specification of synchronization constraints should not prevent method inheritance.

2. It should be possible to inherit, and incrementally modify, synchronization constraints.

The first criterion is important because the need to express method inheritance does not diminish when making the transition from centralized to distributed applications. The second criterion addresses the need to extend inheritance to cover synchronization constraints also. Otherwise, if inheritance applied only to methods, the synchronization constraints for inherited methods would have to be respecified in subclasses, leading to the following problems:

$$pattern \quad ::= \quad method(x_1, \ldots, x_n) \textbf{ if } exp$$
$$constraint \quad ::= \quad \textbf{disable } pattern_1; \ldots; pattern_k$$

Figure 2.1
Abstract syntax for patterns and synchronization constraints

- *Duplication of information.* The same synchronization constraints would be duplicated in the description of multiple classes. Duplication of information makes it harder to maintain programs.

- *Violation of encapsulation.* Because synchronization constraints depend on the private state of objects, respecifying synchronization constraints in the definition of subclasses would expose the representation of superclasses.

In the following, I present the design of language constructs that support synchronization constraints in accordance with the design considerations I have set out. The constructs integrate with inheritance and support separation of synchronization constraints and methods.

2.2   Specification of Synchronization Constraints

The synchronization constraints of an object are a list of *message patterns*. Each pattern prohibits the dispatch of a category of messages—those messages that match the pattern. The programmer defines a pattern within the scope of an object, and a pattern can prohibit the dispatch of only messages destined for that "enclosing" object.

Figure 2.1 introduces the syntax for patterns. The programmer specifies patterns separately from methods as a distinct part of objects. The pattern part of an object is identified by the **disable** keyword.

A pattern "$method(x_1, \ldots, x_n)$ **if** exp" matches a message m if the following two conditions are satisfied:

1. The message m is destined for the method called *method*.

2. The Boolean expression exp evaluates to true in an environment where the *parameters* "$x_1, \ldots, x_n$" are bound to the content of m. Since

a message is a request for invocation of a method, the content of a
message corresponds to the actual values of the invocation.

The parameters of a pattern are similar to the formal parameters of a
function, and the expression of a pattern is similar to the body of a
function. The parameters of a pattern are visible only in the expression
associated with the pattern. Furthermore, the formal parameters of a
pattern must correspond with the parameter list of the method identified
by the pattern. As syntactic sugar, I shall omit the parameter list from a
pattern if the pattern's body expression does not depend on the content
of messages.

The expression of a pattern can refer to the instance variables of the
enclosing object. Thus, pattern matching may depend on the current
state of the enclosing object.

Figure 2.2 illustrates the dispatch of messages when objects are subject to synchronization constraints. When a message arrives at an object, it is stored in the object's input queue. An object can dispatch

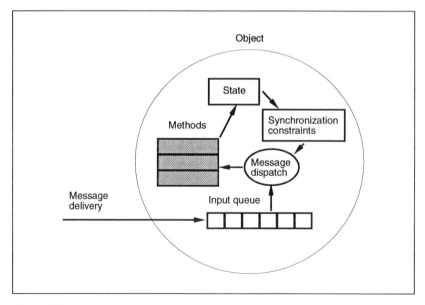

Figure 2.2
An object with synchronization constraints

only those messages in its input queue that do *not* match any of its patterns. If a message matches any pattern, it remains in the input queue. A message that does not match any pattern in its destination object is said to *satisfy* the synchronization constraints of its destination object. Furthermore, a message that satisfies the synchronization constraints of its destination object is said to be *legal*.

The legality of messages may change over time: pattern matching may depend on the state of the enclosing object, and the state of that object can change over time. Hence, a message that matches a pattern at one point in time may not match any pattern at a later point in time. Even if it is not possible to dispatch a message initially, the message may be dispatched later. Since messages can become legal and be dispatched later than their arrival time, the effect of patterns is to delay messages rather than reject them.

Pattern expressions should be free from side effects. If pattern expressions have side effects, the outcome of executing application programs may depend on the order in which pattern expressions are evaluated and on when, and how often, pattern expressions are reevaluated. It is undesirable to have implementation aspects, such as the strategy for expression evaluation, affect the outcome of applications.

I illustrate the notation for synchronization constraints with a simple example:

Example 1 Bounded Buffer
A bounded buffer object has `put` and `get` methods and a `size` instance variable whose value reflects the current number of elements in the buffer. We assume that the bound of a buffer is given by a constant `MAX`; the buffer can hold no more than `MAX` elements. With these conventions, figure 2.3 sketches the structure of a bounded buffer class from which individual buffer objects can be instantiated.

The `item` argument for the `put` method denotes an item to be added to the buffer; the `client` argument of the `get` method denotes a "consumer" object to which the buffer sends an extracted item. The synchronization constraints ensure that a `put` message is not dispatched by a full buffer and that a `get` message is not dispatched by an empty buffer.

Consider the following pattern defined in the `BoundedBuffer` class:

```
put if size = MAX;
```

```
class BoundedBuffer
   size := 0; ...

   disable
     put if size = MAX;
     get if size = 0;
   method put(item) ... end put;
   method get(client) ... end get;
end BoundedBuffer;
```

Figure 2.3
A bounded buffer class

This pattern describes the synchronization constraints for the put method. The pattern matches put messages if the current number of buffer elements is equal to MAX. If the buffer contains fewer than MAX elements, put messages do not match this pattern. Hence, put messages are delayed only if the buffer is full. Since the pattern's body expression (size = MAX) does not depend on the actual items being deposited in the buffer, I have omitted the parameter of the pattern. □

We say that messages satisfy the synchronization constraints of an object if they do not match any pattern in the object. For example, put messages satisfy the synchronization constraints of the bounded buffer if the expression size = MAX evaluates to false. It is important to distinguish between satisfying the synchronization constraints and "satisfying" the Boolean expression of a pattern; these are two opposite notions of satisfaction.

The input queue of an object may contain multiple messages that all satisfy the synchronization constraints of the object. Since messages are dispatched one at a time, a choice must be made between the messages that can be dispatched. Hence, a message is not necessarily dispatched at the first point in time when it satisfies the synchronization constraints. However, the implementation should ensure that a message that continually satisfies the synchronization constraints is eventually dispatched. This notion of fairness can be ensured by recording the arrival order of messages and, when choosing between two messages, dispatching the "oldest" message that satisfies the synchronization constraints. As I discuss in chapter 5, the implementation guarantees this notion of fairness.

2.3   Inheritance of Synchronization Constraints

Inheritance allows a subclass to be defined by incremental modification of a superclass [WZ88]. Traditional inheritance mechanisms provide incremental modification operators for classes and methods. I introduce incremental modification of synchronization constraints.

I employ a simple notion of constraint inheritance: superclass patterns are always inherited, and they are inherited as is. Hence, the synchronization constraints of a subclass consist of the patterns defined in the subclass plus the patterns defined in its superclass.[1] Put more formally, a class C is subject to a pattern P if and only if P satisfies one of the following two conditions:

- P is defined in the **disable** clause of C.

- The superclass of C is subject to P.

These rules imply that patterns are accumulated downward in an inheritance hierarchy; superclass patterns can never be "canceled." Since superclass patterns cannot be canceled, the synchronization constraints of a subclass are at least as restrictive as the synchronization constraints of its superclass. In section 2.4, I examine further the relationship between subclass and superclass synchronization constraints and describe the rationale behind my notion of constraint inheritance.

Since synchronization constraints are specified separately from the constrained methods, it is possible to define subclasses in which only the synchronization constraints are changed.

In the remainder of this section, I present three applications of constraint inheritance. Example 2 is a classic example from the literature on inheritance of synchronization constraints. It illustrates derivation of a subclass with additional methods and refinement of superclass synchronization constraints to handle these additional methods.

Example 2 Bounded Buffer with `get2` Method
Suppose we want to extend the functionality of a bounded buffer by

---

1. For simplicity, we ignore the issue of multiple inheritance.

```
class Get2Buffer inherits BoundedBuffer
  disable get2 if size ≤ 1;
  method get2(client) ... end get2;
end Get2Buffer;
```

Figure 2.4
A bounded buffer subclass

adding a method to retrieve two instead of one element from the buffer.
This extension can be achieved by means of inheritance. A subclass
Get2Buffer can be derived from BoundedBuffer. The Get2Buffer class
inherits put and get from BoundedBuffer, and it defines a get2 method
that sends two elements to a consumer object.

The Get2Buffer class is outlined in figure 2.4. The pattern defined
in Get2Buffer ensures that the get2 method cannot be invoked when
the buffer holds one or fewer elements. With our notion of constraint
inheritance, the synchronization constraints for the get2 method can
be described without interfering with the inheritance of the put and
get methods and their corresponding patterns. As I illustrate in section 2.6.5, this absence of interference is not trivial to obtain. □

The preceding example illustrates inheritance of synchronization constraints for subclasses that add new methods. The following two examples demonstrate the need for actual modification of inherited synchronization constraints.

Example 3 Robot
Consider a computer-controlled robot that moves widgets around in a
workplace. The robot consists of a hand and an arm. The hand grabs
and releases widgets, and the arm moves the hand around. We can model
the robot as a part-whole hierarchy with a robot object that serves as
an "interface" to the hand and arm objects. The hand and arm objects
are then part of the representation of the robot: the outside world only
communicates with the robot object that plays the role of interface.
The robot object defines a method called move that other objects can
invoke in order to move a widget from one position to another. The
move method has two parameters: the start and end positions of a move
operation.

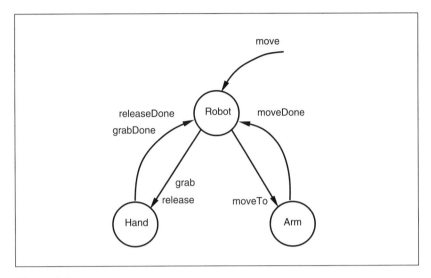

Figure 2.5
A robot object hierarchy

Figure 2.5 illustrates the structure of the robot object hierarchy. In order to service a **move** request, the robot object communicates with the hand and arm objects in order to activate them and cause them to carry out the actual physical movement of a widget. We assume that a hand object responds to **grab** and **release** messages. A hand object sends a **grabDone** message back to the robot object when the actual grab operation is complete at the *physical* robot hand. When it receives a **grabDone** message from its hand object, the robot object knows that it is safe to start moving the physical robot arm. In the same manner, the hand object sends back a **releaseDone** message to the robot object when the physical robot hand is done releasing. The **arm** object responds to **move** messages. In response to a **move** message, the physical robot arm moves the robot hand to a given position in three-dimensional space. When the physical move operation is complete, the arm object sends back a **moveDone** to the robot object.

Suppose that the robot is subject to the following integrity requirements:

- The robot should not move a widget to a position that is already occupied by another widget.

```
class Robot
    active := false;
    hand := ...
    arm := ...
    ...
    disable
      move if active;
      move(from,to) if occupied(to);
    method move(from,to) ... end move;
    method moveDone() ... end moveDone;
    method grabDone() ... end grabDone;
    method releaseDone() ... end releaseDone;
    function occupied(position) ... end occupied;
end Robot;
```

Figure 2.6
A robot class

- While moving a widget, the robot should not start to move another widget. Move requests should be executed serially and not be interleaved.

We can use synchronization constraints for the move method to ensure satisfaction of these integrity requirements. Figure 2.6 sketches the structure of a Robot class that includes these synchronization constraints.

Instances of the Robot class have two instance variables, hand and arm, that refer to the hand and arm objects, respectively. We do not describe instantiation of the hand and arm objects. Since a robot should move only one widget at a time, a robot object should not dispatch additional move messages while it is communicating with the hand and arm objects in response to previous move messages. The variable active indicates whether a robot is currently engaged in a move request. The active variable is initially false. When invoked, the move method sets active to true, and the releaseDone method sets it to false (when the robot object receives a releaseDone message, the current widget movement is complete). The first pattern in the Robot class prevents dispatch of move messages when a robot is busy serving another move request.

The second pattern in the Robot class prevents dispatch of move messages that will result in a collision at the end position. We assume that the robot records the position of widgets that it has moved and that the function occupied determines whether a given position is currently occupied by a widget. Furthermore, we assume that functions, as opposed to methods, in general are free from side effects, and we allow function invocation as part of pattern expressions. In particular, the second pattern invokes the function occupied.

The second pattern in the Robot class also illustrates the use of parameters in a pattern. The pattern parameters from and to are bound to the content of move messages. The content of a move message consists of two values: a start position for a movement and an end position for a movement. The name to is bound to the end position of a movement, and the second pattern's expression uses this end position value as a parameter for the function occupied in order to determine whether this specific position is already occupied.

Now, suppose we want to define a specialized notion of robot that can operate in a physical environment with temporary obstacles. An obstacle may temporarily prevent certain movements of the arm. The robot must keep track of current obstacles and delay move requests that are prevented by the obstacles. We assume the existence of a function obstructed that takes two positions and returns true if moving between these two positions is prevented by the current obstacles. Based on obstructed, figure 2.7 illustrates the structure of a subclass that refines the Robot class to incorporate support for movement in an environment with obstacles.

```
class ObstacleRobot inherits Robot
    disable move(from,to) if obstructed(from,to);
    function obstructed(from,to) ... end obstructed;
    ...
end ObstacleRobot;
```

Figure 2.7
A robot subclass

The subclass defined in figure 2.7 illustrates incremental modification of synchronization constraints. The subclass will inherit the synchronization constraints of the **robot** class, and it will therefore "automatically" satisfy the integrity requirements of the robot hierarchy. The subclass can be defined without explicit reference to, or knowledge of, the synchronization constraints and instance variables defined in the **robot** superclass. Without inheritance, we would have to duplicate the synchronization constraint on **move** as specified in **robot**. Such duplication would expose information that is otherwise encapsulated in the superclass. □

Example 4 Resource Administration
A resource administrator regulates access to shared resources such as disks, processors, or memory. With a resource administrator, the availability of resources is centrally determined. User processes request resources from a resource administrator; a user process invokes a method called **request** in a resource administrator in order to request a number of resources. The parameters of a **request** message specify the type and number of resources requested. User processes send a **release** message to the administrator when they are done using previously requested resources. An administrator should dispatch **request** messages only if the requested resources are available. We can use synchronization constraints to describe this integrity requirement for an administrator.

Figure 2.8 sketches the code for a resource administrator class. The synchronization constraints of an administrator are described by a pat-

```
class ResourceAdministrator
  disable request(client,type,number) if
    (not available(type,number))
  method request(client,type,number) ... end request;
  method release(client,type,number) ... end release;
  function available(type,number) ... end available;
end ResourceAdministrator;
```

Figure 2.8
A resource administrator class

tern that regulates the dispatch of **request** messages. The pattern defined in an administrator calls a function called **available** that determines whether a specified set of resources is currently available. The pattern uses the content of **request** messages as arguments for the call of **available**. By calling **available**, the pattern can determine whether a specific request must be delayed in the current state of the administrator.

Resource administration may introduce deadlocks: two user processes may wait for each other's resources to be released. One way to address this deadlock problem is to avoid the possibility of deadlocks through conservative resource allocation. Deadlock avoidance requires user processes to specify up front the resources that they need during execution. If user processes declare their resource needs up front, the administrator can avoid deadlocks by using the bankers algorithm [SPG91]. Given the expected resource usage of processes, the bankers algorithm can determine whether a given request is safe. A request is safe if it can be granted without introducing the possibility of deadlocks.

We can incrementally modify the resource administrator to incorporate deadlock prevention by the bankers algorithm. A subclass that employs the bankers algorithm is depicted in figure 2.9. This subclass, called **AdministratorWithoutDeadlocks**, strengthens the synchronization constraints for the **request** method: a request for n resources is delayed, even if there are n resources available, if granting the request could lead to a future deadlock.

Notice that, in the subclass, the **request** and **release** methods must

```
class AdministratorWithoutDeadlocks inherits
  ResourceAdministrator
  disable request(client,type,number) if
    (not safe(client,type,number))
  function safe(client,type,number) ... end safe;
  ...
end AdministratorWithoutDeadlocks;
```

Figure 2.9
A resource administrator subclass

be refined so as to maintain the data structures required by the bankers algorithm. These refined methods "extend" the superclass behavior: the basic administration behavior is still part of the refined methods. □

2.4 Refinement of Synchronization Constraints

We analyze the relationship between superclass and subclass synchronization constraints and characterize what it means for synchronization constraints to be refined under inheritance.

Let us first recapitulate the rules for constraint inheritance. With inheritance, a class is subject to both the patterns that it defines itself *and* the patterns that its superclasses define. Specifically, a class C is subject to a pattern P if and only if P satisfies one of the following two conditions:

- P is defined in the **disable** clause of C.
- The superclass of C is subject to P.

For example, if we assume that a superclass is subject to the patterns "$p_1; \ldots; p_n$," and that a subclass defines "$p_{n+1}; \ldots; p_m$," then the subclass is subject to "$p_1; \ldots; p_n; p_{n+1}; \ldots; p_m$." Hence, from a syntactic standpoint, the synchronization constraints of a subclass contains the synchronization constraints of its superclass. In the following I will analyze what this containment relation means at the semantic level.

We can characterize the semantics of synchronization constraints in terms of their effect on incoming messages: whether they delay messages or allow messages to proceed. Remember that a message is delayed by a list of patterns if it matches any pattern in the list. In particular, if a message is delayed by a pattern p, that same message will also be delayed by the list "$p; p'$" for any pattern p'. And in general, if a message is delayed by the list "$p_1, \ldots, p_n$," that message will also be delayed by the list "$p_1, \ldots, p_n, p_{n+1}, \ldots, p_m$." Hence, if a message is delayed by the synchronization constraints in a superclass, it will also be delayed by the synchronization constraints in a subclass. In summary: subclass synchronization constraints are more stringent than superclass synchronization constraints.

With our notion of constraint inheritance, subclass synchronization constraints delay messages at least as often as superclass synchronization constraints. Since synchronization constraints delay messages in order to maintain the integrity of their enclosing object, our notion of constraint inheritance assumes that the integrity of subclasses subsumes the integrity requirements of their superclasses. Integrity subsumption is a reasonable assumption because integrity is a fundamental aspect of the semantics of a class, and if the integrity of a subclass did not subsume the integrity of its superclass, it is questionable whether inheritance is the most descriptive way to capture the relationship between these two classes. In all the examples, the integrity requirements of the subclass subsume the integrity requirements of the superclass.

The simplicity of the notion of constraint inheritance is mainly due to the assumption that subclass integrity subsumes superclass integrity. With this assumption, we can design constructs so that superclass patterns are always inherited and do not need to include constructs for "selective" inheritance of patterns.

2.5   Possible Extensions

The constructs primarily address issues that are related to the integration of synchronization constraints and inheritance. They ignore a number of general issues associated with the description of synchronization constraints. In this section I identify some of these issues and outline a number of extensions to the constructs that address them. We can integrate all the proposed extensions with the basic constructs without interference.

2.5.1   Set-Based Patterns

In my notation, a pattern can constrain only a single method. For example, if we want to constrain n methods, we need to define n patterns. One possible extension would be for patterns to constrain a set of methods rather than single methods.

In order to illustrate the notion of set-based pattern, I illustrate a concrete proposal for such patterns as described in [Frø92]. In this proposal, I used **all-except** and **or** set operators to construct sets of method names.

The expression "**all-except** m" describes a set that contains all methods in the enclosing object *except* the method with name m. A pattern

```
class Lockable
    locked := false;

  disable all-except unlock if locked;
  method lock() locked := true; end lock;
  method unlock() locked := false; end unlock;
end Lockable;
```

Figure 2.10
An abstract lock class

that uses the **all-except** operator can constrain methods without explicitly naming them. For example, consider the class Lockable defined
in figure 2.10. The Lockable class captures the abstract behavior of an
object that can be locked. A lock method locks an object, and the object can be unlocked only by invoking the unlock method. The instance
variable locked is true if the object is locked, and false otherwise.

The **all-except** set operator allows definition of superclass patterns
that can constrain "new" methods added in subclasses. For example,
if a buffer object inherits from Lockable, all the methods in the buffer
object would be constrained by the pattern defined in the Lockable
class. In particular, it is impossible to invoke the buffer's put and get
methods if the variable locked is true. The **all-except** operator allows
the definition of generic synchronization constraints that can be factored
out into abstract superclasses such as the Lockable class.

The **or** operator describes a set by enumeration. For example, the
expression "m **or** n" describes the set { m, n }. We can use the **or**
operator to describe a synchronization constraint that is common to
a number of methods. Consider the Queue class in figure 2.11. The
Queue class has two methods, getFront and getRear, to extract elements from an instance of the Queue class. With the **or** operator we can
directly express that getFront and getRear are subject to the same
synchronization constraint. As for the bounded buffer in example 1, the
variable size keeps track of the current number of elements in a queue
object. Furthermore, the constant MAX denotes the maximum number
of elements that can be stored in a queue.

```
class Queue
    size := 0;

  disable
    getRear or getFront if size = 0;
    put if size = MAX;
  method getRear(client) ... end getRear;
  method getFront(client) ... end getFront;
  method put(item) ... end put;
end Queue;
```

Figure 2.11
A queue class

I do not claim that the **or** and **all-except** operators constitute a suffi-cient means of expressing set-based patterns. I described the functional-ity of these specific operators in order to illustrate concretely the notion of set-based patterns. In practice, more flexibility may be needed. For example, it may be necessary for method names to be first-class values so that a method name can be specified as the result of an expression evaluation rather than as a literal. Moreover, it may be necessary to have sets of method names as first-class values so that the programmer can perform set operations on method set values in addition to method set literals.

2.5.2   Message Priority

Another extension would be to describe priority of messages, that is, user-defined policies for choosing between multiple messages, which can all be dispatched. The built-in dispatch policy is to choose the oldest message, but in some cases the programmer may want to "overwrite" this policy. For example, consider a scheduler object in an operating system. Messages sent to the scheduler represent jobs to be scheduled. If it was possible to have user-defined policies for choosing between messages, the scheduling strategy, such as "shortest job first," could be described as a user-defined dispatch policy. Describing the scheduling strategy as a user-defined dispatch policy has the advantage that the scheduler object does not have to implement a job queue as part of its representation: the input queue of the scheduler object is an implicit job queue.

User-defined dispatch policies could be incorporated directly into our notion of synchronization constraint using a construct similar to **by** in Synchronizing Resources [AOC+88]. The **by** construct is part of **in** statements, which in many ways are similar to input statements in CSP [Hoa78]: objects in SR can explicitly "receive" messages by executing **in** statements. The **by** clause of an **in** statement determines the order in which messages for the same method are received. For example, suppose we want to express the operating system scheduler outlined above. If the scheduler has a `schedule` method to which jobs are sent, the scheduler could receive jobs using an **in** statement of the following form:

in `schedule(job)` **by** `job.length` **ni**

For simplicity we assume that incoming jobs have an attribute `length`, which indicates the length of the job. The expression of a **by** clause must be an arithmetic expression, and the clause causes selectable messages to be received in ascending order of the arithmetic expression. In the above example, the shortest job is received first.

We could incorporate a feature similar to **by** in our language. We could supplement the **disable** clause with a **dispatch** clause that specifies the dispatch policy. With a **dispatch** clause, we could specify message priority separately from the involved methods, along with the synchronization constraints of an object. In figure 2.12, we sketch the structure of a scheduler object where the scheduling strategy is specified with a **dispatch** clause.

The purpose of the discussion is to illustrate the concept of user-defined dispatch policies and to demonstrate, in a concrete way, that

```
class Scheduler
  dispatch schedule(job) by job.length
  method schedule(job) ... end schedule;
end Scheduler;
```

Figure 2.12
A scheduler class

we could extend the notion of synchronization constraint to incorporate the specification of such policies. The **by** construct is an interesting mechanism to specify dispatch policies; I do not discuss its advantages and weaknesses here.

2.5.3   Garbage Collection of Obsolete Messages

Garbage collection of obsolete messages is another possible extension to the notion of synchronization constraint. In some applications, the synchronization constraints will delay certain messages forever. These messages are obsolete since they will never be dispatched. Garbage collecting such messages is a safe operation since it will not change the functionality of applications. Moreover, garbage collection is desirable because it will free wasted space in the input queue.

An example application of garbage collection is a multimedia system where a video monitor displays a stream of video frames in increasing order. The monitor is allowed to skip frames occasionally but should never display old frames. In the multimedia system, it would be desirable to "garbage collect" messages that represent old frames since these messages will never be dispatched.

In some cases, it is possible to infer, by means of static analysis, when particular messages will be obsolete. For example, it may be possible to infer statically that the synchronization constraints of a video monitor are "monotonic" and thereby conclude that old frame messages will be obsolete. However, it is not always possible to determine statically when a given message will be obsolete. For example, the synchronization constraints may depend on program input that is known only at run time. Because it is impossible always to determine statically when a given message is obsolete, the language should provide facilities for the programmer to describe which messages are obsolete. The description of obsolete messages could be accomplished using patterns. A **discard** clause could list a number of patterns with the interpretation that a message matching any pattern in a **discard** clause is obsolete.

Figure 2.13 illustrates the use of a **discard** clause in connection with a video monitor that displays a stream of video frames. The video frames are sent to the method called `display` in the monitor. Each frame has an attribute called `number` that indicates the sequence number of that frame. This attribute makes it possible to avoid showing "old" frames even if frame messages do not arrive in the order that they were sent.

```
class VideoMonitor
    frameNumber := 0;

    discard display(frame) if frame.number < frameNumber;
    method display(frame)
      frameNumber := frame.number;
      ...
    end display;
end VideoMonitor;
```

Figure 2.13
A video monitor with garbage collection of old messages

The video monitor has an instance variable called `frameNumber` that keeps track of the sequence number of the last frame that has been displayed. The **discard** clause contains a pattern that matches "old" messages. A message that matches a pattern in a **discard** clause is not dispatched, and it is eventually garbage collected.

2.6   Related Work

In this section I present other notions of synchronization constraints that have been proposed in the literature.

2.6.1   Semaphores and Monitors

Traditional synchronization constructs, such as semaphores [Dij68] and monitors [Hoa74, Han75], provide a notion of synchronization constraint. With semaphores and monitors, the programmer describes synchronization constraints as actions that conditionally delay the current thread of execution. Semaphores and monitors do not order the way in which messages are dispatched; they order the way in which threads are active within an object.

Monitors are used for synchronization in Mesa [LR80] and Emerald [RTL+91]. The BETA [MPN93] language uses semaphores for synchronization.

With semaphores and monitors, synchronization constraints are described as part of methods. For example, consider a bounded buffer. As we have previously discussed, the `get` method may be executed only if the buffer is not empty. With semaphores or monitors, we cannot prevent invocation of the `get` method. Instead we can design the `get` method so that it can be invoked under all circumstances without causing integrity violations. This can be done by having the `get` method itself test whether the buffer is currently empty and, if so, delay the current thread of execution on a semaphore or, in a monitor, on a condition variable.

Since they describe synchronization constraints as part of methods, semaphores and monitors do not support separation of algorithms and synchronization constraints. Moreover, inheritance of synchronization constraints is subject to the rules for inheritance of methods. In particular, it is not possible to refine the synchronization constraints of an object without changing its methods.

2.6.2   Path Expressions

Path expressions [CH74] is a mechanism for synchronization constraints that specifies the sequences in which a single object can dispatch messages. The programmer specifies these sequences declaratively as regular expressions. A *path* is a regular expression over the method names of a single object. An object can dispatch only message sequences that constitute a string in the language defined by its paths. Numerous languages such as Procol [vdBL91] and SINA [TA88] build on this model for synchronization constraints.

Although specified separately from the constrained methods, path expressions cannot be incrementally modified; a path expression is a monolithic entity.

2.6.3   Receive Actions

In many languages, objects execute special receive actions to allow dispatch of messages. In addition to their methods, objects have a "body" process that executes these receive actions and thereby controls the dispatch of messages. The execution order of receive actions, by the body process, determines the order in which messages can be dispatched.

The use of receive actions is inspired by the communication model used in CSP [Hoa78]. In CSP, processes receive communications by executing input commands. Languages with receive actions include ADA [Uni82], Alps [Vis88], Concurrent Eiffel [Car90], Mediators [GC86], μ-C++ [BSY92], POOL [Ame90], and SR [AOC$^+$88].

Like path expressions, receive actions specify synchronization constraints in terms of the sequences in which messages may be dispatched. Path expressions specify these sequences declaratively and receive actions specify these sequences imperatively. Compared to path expressions, receive actions are less abstract but more flexible.

Languages that describe synchronization constraints as receive actions do not traditionally support incremental modification of synchronization constraints. A notable exception is the language described by Thomsen in [Tho87]. In Thomsen's language, subclass bodies and superclass bodies are executed in quasi-parallel mode as coroutines [Con63]. Because a subclass executes the receive actions defined in the superclass body *and* the receive actions defined in the subclass body, subclasses have more receive actions than superclasses do. Thomsen's language does not support the description of subclasses that restrict the receive actions defined in superclasses; rather, the language supports the description of subclasses that extend the dispatch of messages.

2.6.4   Activation Conditions

An activation condition is a Boolean expression associated with a method. The expression is evaluated prior to invocation of the method, and invocation is allowed only if the expression evaluates to true.

An activation conditions can typically refer to the instance variables of its enclosing object. This is the case in ABCL [Yon90], Maude [Mes93b], and the language proposed in [Shi91]. In some cases, an activation condition can also refer to built-in synchronization "counters" that keep track of the number of ongoing invocations, the number of completed invocations, and the number of messages waiting in the input queue. The concept of synchronization counter was originally proposed by Verjus et al. [BBV78] and is used in Dragoon [AGMB91], Guide [DDR$^+$91], and Scheduling Predicates [MWBD91].

In synchronizing actions [Neu91], activation conditions are part of the interface of objects, and the conditions cannot refer to the instance variables of objects. Instead of instance variables, the activation conditions refer to special *synchronization variables* that are part of the interface and are updated by pre- and postactions associated with methods. The pre- and postactions are also part of the interface. In synchronizing actions, it is possible for an object to expose its synchronization constraints without violating encapsulation.

In the languages mentioned above, the programmer cannot refine the activation conditions for inherited methods. However, a number of recent proposals, such as [Riv95] and [McH94], allow the programmer to redefine the activation conditions for inherited methods. Moreover, since the conditions of a subclass can refer to superclass conditions, it is possible to achieve a notion of condition refinement.

2.6.5   Explicit Method Enabling

Some languages support synchronization constraints as actions that explicitly enable or disable one or more specified methods. An object dispatches messages only for explicitly enabled methods.

In Hybrid [Nie87], each method has an associated delay queue. The language provides actions that can "open" and "close" delay queues. Opening a delay queue enables the corresponding method; closing a delay queue disables the corresponding method.

In Rosette [TS89], ACT++ [KL89], Ellie [And92a, And92b], and the language described by Ishikawa [Ish92], the notion of *enabled set* is used to specify synchronization constraints. An enabled set is a collection of method names. A special action (called **next** in Rosette and **include** in Ellie) installs an enabled set as the current set of enabled methods.

Since *actions* such as **include** and **next** specify synchronization constraints, inheritance of synchronization constraints is influenced by the way in which actions are inherited. In particular, constraint inheritance may interfere with method inheritance.

For example, consider figure 2.14, which sketches a Rosette implementation of a bounded buffer. For pedagogic reasons, the example is described in the same syntax as the rest of the examples. I use [...] to describe an enabled set. The statement **next[get]** enables the set consisting of the **get** method.

Now suppose we want to derive a subclass `Get2Buffer`, similar to the class mentioned in example 2, which adds a method, `get2`, to retrieve two buffer elements rather than one. In defining the `Get2Buffer` subclass of `BoundedBuffer`, we want to inherit the `put` and `get` methods. But with enabled sets, this is not possible; the problem is that we need to change the **if** statement in the `get` method in order to take the `get2` method

```
class BoundedBuffer
    size := 0; ...

  method put(item)
    ...
    if size = MAX then
      next([get]);
    else
      next([put,get]);
    end put;

  method get(client)
    ...
    if size = 0 then
      next([put]);
    else
      next([put,get]);
    end get;
end BoundedBuffer;
```

Figure 2.14
A bounded buffer class that is specified with enabled sets

into account, and the only way to change this statement is to redefine
the get method.

My notation avoids the problem of method redefinition because synchronization constraints and methods are described separately. The separation of methods and synchronization constraints makes it possible to
refine synchronization constraints independently of methods; it is never
necessary to change methods in order to change synchronization constraints.

2.6.6   Hybrid Approaches

The proposal outlined in [MTY93] defines a hybrid approach to synchronization constraints. The proposal incorporates activation conditions as
well as explicit method enabling. The foundation of the proposal is the

notion of a method set, which is a set of method names. Method sets can be named and redefined in subclasses. An activation condition specifies a condition that enables a method set. Activation conditions are specified separately from the methods and can be redefined in subclasses. Finally, a notion of explicit enabling is supported by *transition specifications*. A transition specification identifies the set of methods to be enabled after invocation of a particular method. In contrast to Rosette, transition specifications can be redefined in subclasses since they are described declaratively, separately from methods. The proposal does not support synchronization constraints that depend on the content of incoming messages.

2.7 Conclusion

Our language constructs support object-oriented synchronization constraints. It is essential for object-oriented synchronization constraints to satisfy the following properties:

- *Separation.* Synchronization constraints should be specified separately from the methods being constrained. First, methods and synchronization constraints are logically distinct aspects: methods describe *how* objects respond to messages, and synchronization constraints describe *when* objects respond to messages. Second, separating synchronization constraints from methods allows us to define different and independent inheritance mechanisms for synchronization constraints and methods. The independence of constraint inheritance and method inheritance is the key to integration of inheritance and synchronization constraints.

- *Incremental modification.* Since inheritance is an essential part of object-oriented programming, inheritance should also be available for synchronization constraints. Extending inheritance to cover synchronization constraints requires that synchronization constraints can be incrementally modified. As the examples show, it must be possible for subclasses to refine the synchronization constraints applicable to superclass methods.

I believe that the principles underlying the constructs are general purpose and that they can be applied to most concurrent, object-oriented languages. Clearly, the idiosyncrasies of a specific host language will influence the concrete manifestation of patterns in that language. For example, virtual methods in the BETA language [MPN93] can refine their parameter list under inheritance: the parameter list of a subclass method can be an extension of the parameter list of a superclass method. If method parameter lists can be extended, it should also be possible to extend pattern parameter lists.

Inheritance of synchronization constraints is an active area of research. The more recent proposals, such as [MTY93, Riv95, McH94], emphasize flexibility in the derivation of subclass synchronization constraints. In these proposals, it is possible to strengthen, weaken, and totally cancel superclass synchronization constraints. However, there is a direct relation between flexibility and complexity of the introduced constructs. Rather than support all possible constraint modifications under inheritance, my goal is to introduce a set of simple constructs that support the way in which inheritance is typically used in practice. In particular, I support modifications that result in more stringent subclass synchronization constraints. This design decision is based on the assumption that subclasses are subject to the same semantic integrity requirements as superclasses. It is my experience that this assumption is satisfied in practice. If this assumption is satisfied, the constructs capture the derivation of synchronization constraints in a simpler and more direct manner than the alternative proposals, which emphasize greater flexibility.

3 Synchronizers

A synchronizer maintains the integrity of a group of objects by ensuring that message dispatch within the group occurs in a certain user-specified order. With synchronizers, the programmer can express the integrity of an object group as a distinct entity rather than as part of the individual group members. The separation of group properties and the individual properties of group members promotes reuse and modularity and allows the programmer to express the logical structure of distributed applications more clearly.

Synchronizers and synchronization constraints describe integrity at different levels. Synchronization constraints describe the integrity of individual objects; synchronizers describe the integrity of object groups. These different levels of integrity give rise to different language constructs with different design goals.

I introduce language constructs that support synchronizers and use these constructs to express group-level integrity requirements of example applications. I discuss the constructs and identify possible extensions and alternatives.

3.1 Design Considerations

It should be possible to enforce synchronizers on existing objects in a manner that is *transparent* to the objects themselves. Transparency means that objects do not have to anticipate the presence of synchronizers. In particular, synchronizers should enforce ordering constraints without explicit communication with the constrained objects.

Transparency enables reuse of distributed objects. Building applications by composing generic objects is an important aspect of reuse. When composing *distributed* objects, it is often necessary to coordinate their activities. For example, as I described in chapter 1, composing a multimedia system from an audio device and a video device requires coordination of the two devices. But if we want to reuse generic audio and video devices, the required coordination must be enforced transparently.

Transparency requires *separation*, which is another design goal. Separation means that synchronizers are described as distinct entities separately from the objects that they constrain. Transparency requires separation because synchronizers cannot be transparent if they are described as part of the objects that they constrain.

Group properties and the properties of individual objects are different
design concerns of a distributed application. Separation gives *modularity*
because these different design concerns are described as distinct entities.
Moreover, describing group-level ordering constraints separately from
objects makes it easier to reason about such constraints; one can reason
about the constraints without being concerned with, or distracted by,
the internal representation of objects.

Synchronizers should rely only on object *interfaces*, not the internal representation of objects. Using object interfaces as an abstraction
boundary between objects and synchronizers has two advantages:

- *Encapsulation.* If synchronizers could refer directly to the internal
  representation of objects, they would violate object encapsulation. A
  synchronizer is a distinct entity, and if it could refer directly to the
  internal representation of an object, it would expose this representation to the world outside the object. Having interfaces as abstraction
  boundaries prevents violation of object encapsulation.

- *Reuse.* We can apply the same synchronizer to different objects if the
  objects have compatible interfaces.

We want to support *composition* of synchronizers. It should be possible for multiple synchronizers to overlap, that is, constrain the same
group of objects. Composition enables a complex message-ordering constraint to be constructed from multiple simpler pieces that are specified
separately. Furthermore, composition supports *evolution*: existing synchronizers can be supplemented by new synchronizers that apply to the
same objects.

3.2   Synchronizers and Synchronization Constraints

Synchronization constraints express the integrity requirements of individual objects; synchronizers express the integrity requirements of object groups. One could argue that the functionality of synchronizers
subsumes the functionality of synchronization constraints and that synchronization constraints should be described as single-object synchronizers. The argument for why it is useful to have two distinct constructs
is as follows.

Suppose that synchronizers took the place of synchronization constraints and that we used them to express the integrity requirements of single objects. Since an object's integrity may depend on its internal representation, and since synchronizers, according to the design goals, cannot refer directly to this representation, synchronizers would then need to "duplicate" the representation of objects. This duplication would expose the internal representation of objects and thereby violate their encapsulation. Furthermore, duplication would lead to double bookkeeping of the current state of objects. The conclusion is that having both synchronizers and synchronization constraints is necessary in order to maintain the abstraction boundary defined by object interfaces.

3.3   Functionality of Synchronizers

Synchronizers are similar to objects in that they have a private encapsulated state. Unlike objects, synchronizers neither send nor receive messages. Instead, a synchronizer observes and constrains the dispatch of messages at "ordinary" objects.

The functionality of a synchronizer is specified in terms of triggers and constraints. A *trigger* observes the message dispatch at a specific object, and it executes an action when this object dispatches certain messages. The action of a trigger can change the state of its "enclosing" synchronizer. A synchronizer can contain multiple triggers, and the state of a synchronizer can reflect the collective invocation history of a group of objects.

A synchronizer can have two kinds of constraints: *atomicity constraints* that guarantee indivisible dispatch of multiple messages by multiple objects and *disabling constraints* that provide conditional dispatch of individual messages. Atomicity and disabling constraints can be used to describe different kinds of dependencies between the dispatch actions performed by a group of objects.

Atomicity constraints can be used to describe *mutual* dependencies between dispatch actions. For example, if a and b are two messages destined for two different objects, an atomicity constraint can specify that a cannot be dispatched unless b is dispatched, and that b cannot be dispatched unless a is dispatched. Mutual dependencies of this kind capture situations where a set of messages must be dispatched so that either all or none of the messages are dispatched, and where it must never be the case that only part of the set is dispatched.

Disabling constraints can be used to describe *one-way* dependencies between dispatch actions. For example, if a and b are two messages at two different objects, a disabling constraint can be used to specify that a must be dispatched before b. These one-way dependencies capture temporal ordering of dispatch actions across objects.

A disabling constraint is similar to synchronization constraints in that it can be used to specify temporal ordering of dispatch actions. Unlike synchronization constraints, disabling constraints can be used to specify temporal ordering at the object-group level, across individual objects.

The behavior of both triggers and constraints can depend on the current state of the enclosing synchronizer. Since triggers can update the state of their enclosing synchronizer, the behavior of triggers and constraints can be history sensitive, that is, it can depend on messages that were dispatched in the past.

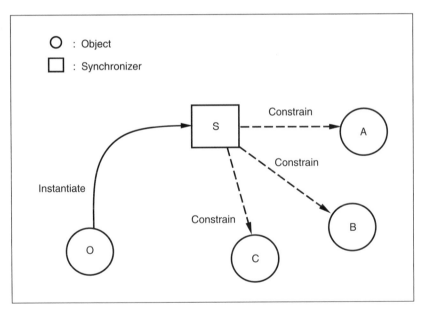

Figure 3.1
Synchronizer instantiation

Synchronizers are instantiated by objects. Instantiating a synchronizer enforces message-ordering constraints on a group of objects. Figure 3.1 illustrates a scenario where an object o instantiates a synchronizer s in order to enforce a constraint on the objects a, b, and c. In order for s to constrain a, b, and c, s must have a reference to those objects. These references are passed to s by o when o instantiates s.

At the language level, instantiation of s is transparent to the objects a, b, and c; at the implementation level, instantiation of s involves communication with these objects. In many cases, the object o may want to determine when s is "fully instantiated." Determining when s is fully instantiated will enable o to send messages to a, b, and c knowing that these messages are constrained by s. As a consequence, synchronizer instantiation takes place according to a request-reply style protocol where a synchronizer sends back an implicit acknowledgment to the instantiating object when the instantiation process is complete.

3.4 Language Support for Synchronizers

I present language constructs that provide a concrete form to the principles behind synchronizers and facilitate the description of example applications. I have striven for simplicity in the language design in order to focus on the essential aspects of synchronizers.

I describe the behavior of synchronizers using the notation in figure 3.2. A synchronizer is instantiated from a synchronizer *template*.

$$
\begin{aligned}
&\textbf{synchronizer } name(par_1, \ldots, par_n) \\
&\quad var_1 := exp_1; \\
&\quad \ldots \\
&\quad var_k := exp_k; \\
&\quad relation_1; \\
&\quad \ldots \\
&\quad relation_m; \\
&\textbf{end } name
\end{aligned}
$$

Figure 3.2
Notation for synchronizer behavior

The relationship between a synchronizer template and synchronizers instantiated from the template is similar to the relationship, in object-oriented programming, between a class and the objects instantiated from that class.

The functionality of a synchronizer is specified by a number of relations. A relation is either a trigger or a constraint. Similar to a procedure, a synchronizer template has a set of parameters; and similar to a class, a synchronizer template has instance variables. When an object instantiates a synchronizer from a template, it provides actual values that are bound to the formal parameters par_i of the template. The parameter mechanism for synchronizer templates is similar to traditional procedure activation. After the parameter bindings have been established, the expressions exp_j are evaluated, and the resulting values are bound to the instance variables var_j. The binding of values to the instance variables initializes the state of the instantiated synchronizer.

It is possible to instantiate synchronizers that overlap, that is, constrain the same objects. Modulo name conflicts, the semantics of instantiating a synchronizer with relations "r_1 ; ... ; r_n" *and* a synchronizer with relations "r_{n+1} ; ... ; r_m," is the same as instantiating a synchronizer with relations "r_1 ; ... ; r_n ; r_{n+1} ; ... ; r_m." However, it may simplify the construction and maintenance of distributed applications to instantiate several simple synchronizers rather than one complex synchronizer.

In the following I shall not always distinguish between synchronizer templates and synchronizer instances and use the term *synchronizer* for both kinds of entities unless it is necessary to make an explicit distinction.

In the remainder of this section, I describe the syntax and informal semantics of constraints and triggers and give prototypical examples of their use. The abstract syntax for constraints and triggers is given in figure 3.3.

3.4.1   Message Patterns

Both constraints and triggers are described in terms of message patterns. A message pattern identifies a set of messages based on pattern matching. The pattern "$o.n(x_1, ..., x_n)$ **if** e" matches all messages m that satisfy the following two conditions:

$$
\begin{array}{rcl}
relation & ::= & trigger \\
 & | & constraint \\
constraint & ::= & \textbf{disable } pattern \\
 & | & \textbf{atomic}(pattern_1, \ldots, pattern_n) \\
trigger & ::= & \textbf{trigger } pattern \rightarrow actions \\
pattern & ::= & object.method(name_1, \ldots, name_n) \textbf{ if } exp
\end{array}
$$

Figure 3.3
Abstract syntax for patterns, constraints, and triggers

1. The destination of m is the method n in the object o. Notice that o is a specific instance of a class. The object o is called the *destination* of the pattern.

2. The expression e must evaluate to true in a binding context where the parameters "$x_1, \ldots, x_n$" are bound to the content of m. The message m is a request for invocation of the method n, and the content of m is the parameter values of the invocation. The parameters "$x_1, \ldots, x_n$" correspond to the formal parameters of the method n. The expression e is an arbitrary user-defined expression.[1]

The second condition allows pattern matching to depend on the content of messages. The parameters of a pattern are similar to the formal parameters of a function. Where functions are applied to values, patterns are applied to messages.

A pattern is scoped within a synchronizer and the expression of a pattern can refer to the instance variables of the enclosing synchronizer. Since the state of a synchronizer can change over time, pattern matching is history sensitive: whether a given message matches a given pattern can depend on the invocation history of objects.

The expression of a pattern should not have side effects; that is, it should not change the instance variables of the enclosing synchronizer. The state of a synchronizer should be mutated only by the triggers defined in the synchronizer.

---

1. This means that expression evaluation may not terminate. I discuss the semantics and implications of this on page 103.

As syntactic sugar, I will omit the list of parameters from a pattern that does not refer to the content of messages. Similarly, I omit the expression from a pattern that refers neither to the content of messages nor to the state of the enclosing synchronizer.

The notion of pattern introduced above is conceptually similar to the notion of pattern introduced in chapter 2. The patterns introduced above extend the notion of pattern introduced in chapter 2 by explicitly identifying the "destination object" of messages. In chapter 2, patterns were described within the scope of individual objects, and the destination object was always the enclosing object. With synchronizers, this notion of pattern is not sufficient because synchronizer patterns are external to objects, and they have no enclosing object.

3.4.2 Triggers

A trigger of the form "**trigger** $p \rightarrow$ *actions*" will execute the actions in *actions* each time an object dispatches a message that matches p. The actions of a trigger may contain arbitrary statements. In particular, the actions may assign to the instance variables of the enclosing synchronizer. In order to avoid deadlocks, trigger actions should be nonblocking, for example, without request-reply style communication. The trigger actions in the examples only mutate the state of synchronizers; they do not communicate with the outside world. By means of state mutation, synchronizers can record the invocation history of objects. Because the state mutation is user defined, the state of a synchronizer is an encoded, rather than a direct, representation of the relevant invocation history.

Since the same message can match the pattern of multiple triggers in the same synchronizer, we need to introduce concurrency control at synchronizers. If the same message causes execution of multiple trigger actions in the same synchronizer, these actions are executed serially, and the order of serial execution is nondeterministic.

3.4.3 Disabling Constraints

A constraint of the form "**disable** p" prevents dispatch of any message that matches p. A message that cannot be dispatched is kept in the input queue of its destination object. We say that a message *satisfies* a disabling constraint if it does not match the constraint's pattern.

Because pattern matching can depend on the state of synchronizers, messages that cannot be dispatched at one point in time may be dispatched later when they are no longer matched by any pattern in a disabling constraint. A combination of triggers and disabling constraints can enforce ordering between messages; the state changes caused by triggers can "switch" the disabling constraints on and off through state-dependent pattern matching.

In order to increase the clarity and brevity of the examples, I introduce the following syntactic conventions.

- In general, a relation has a keyword that indicates its kind and a body that specifies its functionality. For example, the relation "**disable** p" has the keyword **disable** and the body p. When specifying a number of relations of the same kind, I shall sometimes omit the keyword from all but the first relation. For example, I use the following shorthand for disabling constraints:

  disable $p_1; \ldots; p_n$ $\equiv$ **disable** $p_1; \ldots;$ **disable** p_n

  I use similar shorthands for triggers and atomicity constraints.

- If the list l contains the objects $o_1, \ldots, o_n$ that each has a method m, I use the following shorthand to define constraints and triggers for $o_1.m, \ldots, o_n.m$:

  for o **in** l : **disable** $o.m$ $\equiv$ **disable** $o_1.m; \ldots; o_n.m$

  for o **in** l : **trigger** $o.m \to a$ $\equiv$ **trigger** $o_1.m \to a; \ldots; o_n.m \to a$

  This notation makes it more convenient to specify the same relation for a set of objects. Without this shorthand, I would have to specify a separate relation for each object in a set; with this shorthand one single relation can apply to the entire set of objects. The shorthand is not "pure" syntactic sugar since it cannot be expanded statically (it may be impossible to determine statically the objects in l). However, the shorthand is purely syntactic: it does not introduce a new concept, only a new way to describe an existing concept.

I use these syntactic conventions in the following example, which illustrates the semantics of triggers and disabling constraints in terms of distributed mutual exclusion.

```
class Button
     isOn := false;

  disable
     on   if isOn;
     off if not isOn;
  method on()   isOn := true;  ... end on;
  method off()  isOn := false; ... end off;
end Button;
```

Figure 3.4
A button class

Example 5 Distributed Mutual Exclusion
A button can be switched on and off; a set of radio buttons must furthermore satisfy the property that at most one button is switched on at any time. The notion of radio buttons illustrates distributed mutual exclusion: switching one button on excludes all other buttons from being switched on.

Each button can be implemented as an object with **on** and **off** methods. A button object is subject to the integrity requirement that the **on** and **off** methods must be invoked in alternation. For example, it should not be possible to invoke the **on** method twice without an inter-leaving invocation of the **off** method. Since this integrity requirement is associated with individual buttons, it should be described as a synchronization constraint. I describe the structure of a **Button** class in figure 3.4. The instance variable **isOn** indicates whether a button is on or off. Initially, a button is switched off.

The mutual exclusion associated with radio buttons is a property of a group of buttons rather than individual buttons. As sketched in figure 3.5, we can describe this property by a synchronizer.

The synchronizer in figure 3.5 constrains a group of buttons and ensures that the group behaves as radio buttons. When the synchronizer is instantiated, it is passed a set of objects as an actual parameter. The objects in this set constitute the group of buttons. Inside the synchronizer, the set is bound to the parameter called **buttons**. The instance variable **activated** is the state of the synchronizer. The value of **activated** is

```
synchronizer radioButtons(buttons)
    activated := false;

  for b in buttons :
    trigger
        b.on  → { activated := true; };
        b.off → { activated := false; };
  for b in buttons :
    disable
        b.on if activated;
end radioButtons;
```

Figure 3.5
A synchronizer that provides mutual exclusion for radio buttons

true if any button is switched on and false if all buttons are switched off. Initially, the value of `activated` is false. The two trigger relations update the value of `activated` when a button is switched either on or off. The disabling constraints enforce mutual exclusion among the buttons: if any button is switched on, `activated` is true, and dispatch of on messages is prevented because they match the pattern "`b.on if activated`." When the button is switched off again, the value of `activated` is changed to true by the triggers, and dispatch of on messages will no longer be prevented.

The `radioButtons` synchronizer enforces message ordering by a combination of triggers and disabling constraints; execution of a trigger affects the value of the `activated` variable, which influences the pattern matching performed as part of the disabling constraints. □

In the radio button example, buttons are subject to both synchronization constraints and a synchronizer. As illustrated by the example, synchronization constraints can be used to describe integrity requirements that are an inherent part of objects. For example, the requirement that on and off messages must be dispatched in strict alternation is an inherent part of a button, and it is a requirement that must be satisfied regardless of the button's context. I use synchronization constraints to describe this requirement as part of buttons. Synchronizers can be used to describe group-level integrity requirements. For example, the requirement that at most one button in a group can be switched on at any time is a requirement of the group rather than a requirement of individual buttons in the group. One could easily imagine another group of buttons without this requirement. I use a synchronizer to describe the radio button property as part of a group of buttons rather than as part of the individual buttons.

The presence of both synchronizers and synchronization constraints makes it possible to specify integrity requirements as part of the entity to which they logically belong. Moreover, the constructs offer an integrated approach to the specification of both kinds of integrity requirements: both synchronization constraints and synchronizers use the notion of message pattern, and both constructs specify integrity requirements in the form of message-ordering constraints.

There is a two-way relationship between synchronizers and objects: synchronizers can influence the dispatch of messages at objects, and the dispatch of messages at objects can trigger state changes at synchronizers. For a given message, these two effects must occur as an atomic action without any observable middle states. It must appear as if testing disabling constraints, possibly dispatching the message, and triggering the state change at synchronizers all take place as *one* indivisible action.

Since it is an atomic action to dispatch a message at an object and observe this dispatch at a synchronizer, the order in which messages are observed at synchronizers is consistent with the order in which messages are dispatched at objects.

3.4.4   Atomicity Constraints

An atomicity constraint prevents certain messages from being dispatched individually and requires that they are dispatched along with other messages as an atomic action. An atomicity constraint captures integrity requirements where the dispatch of a message by one object requires the dispatch of other messages by other objects.

A message that matches a pattern in any atomicity constraint cannot be dispatched individually; it can be dispatched only as part of a message set that satisfies an atomicity constraint. A set of n messages satisfies the constraint "**atomic**$(p_1, \ldots, p_n)$" if and only if the following two conditions are satisfied:

1. Each of the n messages matches *exactly* one of the message patterns
   "$p_1, \ldots, p_n$."
2. Each of the n messages is destined for a different object.

Without the second condition we would need to implement a notion of
"undo" for message dispatch. For example, assume that a message set
contains two messages, say m_1 and m_2, that are destined for the same
object, say o. Assume further that this message set is to be dispatched as
an atomic action. Since m_1 and m_2 are both destined for o, one of these
messages will be dispatched before the other. If m_1 is dispatched before
m_2, m_1 could change the state of o and thereby cause o's synchronization
constraints to prevent dispatch of m_2. But if m_2 cannot be dispatched,
we need to undo the dispatch of m_1: the atomicity constraint requires
that either all or none of the messages be dispatched. The problem is
that with multiple messages destined for the same object, we cannot a
priori determine the legality of all messages.

   Since we require that multiple messages cannot be destined for the
same object, we do not need any notion of rollback or undo: the possibility of dispatching the entire message set can be determined before any
message is dispatched. Not having to incorporate a notion of rollback
enables a more efficient implementation.

   Dispatch of a message m that matches an atomicity constraint depends on the availability of other messages. The dispatch of m is delayed
unless messages are available at other objects so that m and these other
messages constitute a message set that satisfies an atomicity constraint.

   We use the classical dining philosophers problem to illustrate the functionality of atomicity constraints.

Example 6 Dining Philosophers
A group of philosophers (processes) need to coordinate their access
to a number of chopsticks (resources). The number of chopsticks and
the number of philosophers is the same, and a philosopher needs two
chopsticks in order to eat. Access to the chopsticks needs to be regulated
in order to avoid deadlock and starvation.

   We can represent philosophers and chopsticks as distributed objects.
We sketch the structure of a `Chopstick` class in figure 3.6. A chopstick
object has a `pickup` method and a `drop` method. Philosophers invoke
the `pickup` method in order to pick up a chopstick. The argument,

```
class Chopstick
    isPicked := false;

  disable pickup if isPicked;
  method pickup(phil) isPicked := true; ... end pickup;
  method drop() isPicked := false; ... end drop;
end Chopstick;
```

Figure 3.6
A chopstick class

phil, of pickup is a reference to the philosopher making the request.
Philosophers invoke the drop method when they are done using the
chopstick.

A chopstick can be used by only one philosopher at a time. We model
this integrity requirement as a property of chopsticks and represent it
as a synchronization constraint for chopsticks. The instance variable
isPicked indicates whether a chopstick is currently in use by a philosopher. The synchronization constraint of a chopstick prevents invocation
of pickup if isPicked is true.

If philosophers could pick up one chopstick at a time, it would be
possible to end up with a deadlocked system where each philosopher has
one chopstick. In order to prevent this scenario, each philosopher should
pick up two chopsticks as an indivisible action. This indivisibility can
be achieved by enforcing an atomicity constraint on the invocation of
pickup methods: pickup messages can only be dispatched in atomic
pairs, guaranteeing that a philosopher never gets only one chopstick.

The synchronizer in figure 3.7 enforces the necessary atomicity constraint on the way in which a philosopher phil accesses two chopsticks
c1 and c2. The atomicity constraint prevents dispatch of individual
pickup messages. At the same time, the atomicity constraint facilitates
collective and indivisible dispatch of two pickup messages—one destined
for c1 and one destined for c2. Furthermore, the atomicity constraint
ensures that collective dispatch occurs only if the two messages are sent
by the same philosopher.

The synchronizer in figure 3.7 coordinates the access to chopsticks for

```
synchronizer indivisiblePickup(c1,c2,phil)
  atomic
    (c1.pickup(p1) if p1 = phil,
     c2.pickup(p2) if p2 = phil);
end indivisiblePickup;
```

Figure 3.7
A synchronizer that enforces indivisible access to multiple chopsticks

one philosopher. In order to obtain a complete solution to the dining philosophers problem, one such synchronizer must be instantiated for each philosopher with his associated chopsticks. Together these synchronizers will enforce an access scheme that is free from deadlocks. It should be noted that freedom from starvation is guaranteed by the fairness of the underlying implementation. □

The dining philosophers example illustrates a scenario with overlapping synchronizers. Each philosopher has an associated synchronizer that orders the dispatch of `pickup` messages at the two chopsticks accessed by the philosopher. But since each chopstick is accessed by two philosophers, it will be constrained by two synchronizers. These two synchronizers overlap because they constrain a common chopstick object. The overlapping synchronizers give rise to overlapping atomicity constraints, and in the following I describe the semantics of overlapping atomicity constraints.

The overlap of synchronizers in the dining philosophers example is illustrated in figure 3.8. We associate an index with each philosopher and chopstick. Philosopher i accesses chopstick i and $i + 1$, and chopstick i is shared between philosopher $i - 1$ and philosopher i. In the figure, a synchronizer is depicted as a dashed line around the group of objects that it coordinates. Each synchronizer in the dining philosophers example coordinates an object group consisting of a philosopher and two chopsticks. Each synchronizer enforces an atomicity constraint on the two chopsticks.

Because the synchronizers in the dining philosophers example overlap, a `pickup` message sent to chopstick i will be subject to two atomicity constraints: one associated with philosopher $i - 1$ and one associated

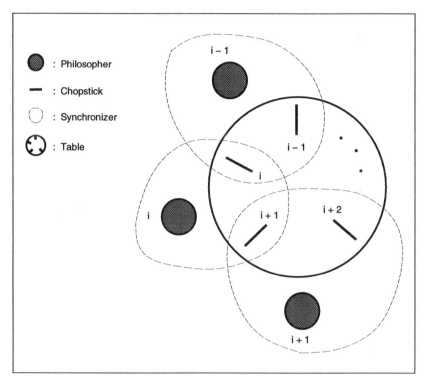

Figure 3.8
Overlapping synchronizers in the dining philosophers example

with philosopher i. Each of these constraints defines a possible message
set for this `pickup` message: it can pair with a `pickup` message for
chopstick $i - 1$ and thereby satisfy the first atomicity constraint, *or* it
can pair with a `pickup` message for chopstick $i + 1$ and thereby satisfy
the second atomicity constraint. If both possibilities exist—there is both
a `pickup` message for $i - 1$ and a `pickup` message for $i + 1$—the choice
between these two possibilities is nondeterministic.

As illustrated by the dining philosophers example, an atomicity constraint has a preventing as well as an enabling aspect. On one hand,
an atomicity constraint prevents individual dispatch of messages that
match any of its patterns. On the other hand, an atomicity constraint
enables indivisible dispatch of a message set that satisfies the constraint.

3.4.5   Composing Disabling and Atomicity Constraints

The preceding sections have discussed disabling constraints and atomicity constraints in isolation. However, the same synchronizer may define both disabling and atomicity constraints. This section discusses the composite effect of atomicity and disabling constraints.

Both atomicity constraints and disabling constraints define conditions for message dispatch: disabling constraints define conditions based on Boolean expressions, and atomicity constraints define conditions based on availability of other messages. For a message to be dispatched, it must satisfy all applicable conditions whether, defined as part of disabling or atomicity constraints. In particular, for a message m to be dispatched, it must satisfy the following two criteria:

- m must not match the pattern of any disabling constraint in any synchronizer.

- Either m does not match any pattern in any atomicity constraint in any synchronizer *or* m is part of a message set that satisfies an atomicity constraint in a synchronizer.

For example, consider the synchronizer composed in figure 3.9. A message destined for the method m in object o is subject to two conditions: the expression exp must be false *and* the object p must have a message in its input queue that is destined for the method called n.

```
synchronizer composed(o,p)
    disable o.m if exp;
    atomic(o.m,p.n);
end composed;
```

Figure 3.9
Composition of constraints

Constraint composition may yield conditions that are impossible to satisfy. The consequence of an unsatisfiable condition is that certain messages remain in the input queue forever. For example, if the expression exp in figure 3.9 is equal to the value true, messages destined for the method m would remain in o's input queue forever. But this does not mean that all messages destined for o are blocked; an unsatisfiable condition does not deadlock the system.

The possibility of blocking messages forever is not specific to synchronizers. Infinite blocking of messages would also be possible if the programmer implemented message-ordering constraints in an ad hoc manner. One significant advantage of using synchronizers instead of ad hoc implementation techniques is that dispatch conditions are specified separately and not as part of objects. This makes it easier for the programmer to comprehend constraints in general and the ramifications of constraint composition in particular.

3.5   Combined Evaluation

The same message may be constrained by both synchronization constraints and synchronizers. This was the case in example 5, where a group of radio buttons was constructed from individual buttons. Each button had an on and off method, and on messages were constrained by both synchronization constraints at individual buttons and a synchronizer at the object-group level.

For an object to dispatch a message, the message must satisfy the object's synchronization constraints and all constraints defined in synchronizers. Moreover, a message must satisfy the synchronization constraints and the synchronizer constraints at the same time, namely, when the message is dispatched; evaluating the synchronization constraints, evaluating the synchronizer constraints, and dispatching the message must be one atomic and indivisible action.

The need for combined evaluation of synchronization constraints and synchronizer constraints complicates the implementation. For example, we cannot implement synchronizers as part of the communication subsystem. It is not sufficient to ensure that messages are delivered in an order that is consistent with the constraints in synchronizers. Even if messages were delivered in a correct order, the synchronization constraints may delay and reorder messages and cause messages to be dispatched in an order that is different from the order in which they were delivered, thereby potentially violating the constraints in synchronizers. Although synchronizers are transparent to objects at the language level, objects need to know about synchronizers at the implementation level. Otherwise we cannot ensure that synchronization constraints and synchronizer constraints are satisfied at the same time. In chapter 5, I describe an implementation where evaluating the synchronization constraints, evaluating the synchronizer constraints, and dispatching a message is one atomic and indivisible action.

Since message-ordering constraints are inherent in distributed applications, their implementation is not optional; message-ordering constraints must be implemented at some level, in either an ad hoc manner by the programmer or in a generic manner by the language run-time system. The need for combined and atomic evaluation of message-ordering constraints at the per-object level (synchronization constraints) and message-ordering constraints at the object-group level (synchronizers) makes it complicated for the programmer to construct an ad hoc implementation. Hence, it is important to provide language support for message-ordering constraints and implement them as part of the language run-time system, thereby hiding the implementation complexity from the programmer. Moreover, it is important that a language supports *both* synchronizers and synchronization constraints. If only one of these concepts were provided in a language, the programmer would have to implement the other in an ad hoc manner. The ad hoc implementation would be complicated because the programmer would then have to ensure atomicity of the combination of the ad hoc implementation and the run-time system implementation.

3.6   Application of Synchronizers

Having described the syntax and informal semantics of synchronizers, I now proceed to outline example applications of synchronizers.

Example 7 Coordinating Robots
In example 2, I outlined the structure of a robot, a composite object with hand and arm parts. In moving a widget, the robot activated the hand and arm objects in order to perform the actual movement. The robot moved only one widget at a time, and two widgets could not occupy the same position. I captured these integrity requirements as synchronization constraints in the robot object.

Suppose that we want to compose two robots in a way that allows them to share widgets. In order to share widgets, there must be a position

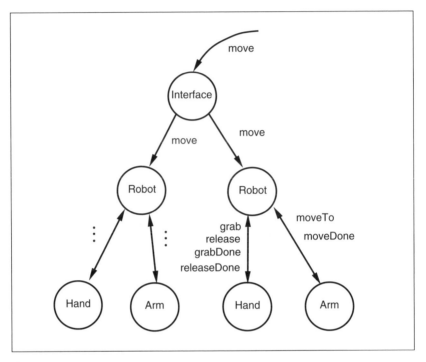

Figure 3.10
Composed robots with a top-level object that serves as interface

that both robots can reach. Sharing involves *cross-robot movement* of widgets: one robot first moves a widget to the shared area; the other robot then grabs the widget in the shared area and moves it to the end position. A cross-robot movement is one logical activity implemented by two separate **move** operations—one performed by each robot.

I introduce a top-level object that is an interface to the composed robots. As illustrated in figure 3.10, the resulting system is an object hierarchy in three levels: the top-level object is the highest level, the next level is the interface of the individual robots, and the bottom level is the hand and arm components of individual robots. Clients send move requests to the top-level object, and the top-level object activates one or both robots depending on whether the move request requires cross-robot movement. The top-level object represents one logical robot that can serve all move requests within the combined scope of the two robots.

The world external to the composed robots need not be concerned about which robot(s) actually implement a specific move request.

The composed robots constitute an object group that is subject to the following group-level integrity requirements:

- *Totality.* When initiating a cross-robot movement, the top-level object sends a move message to both robots. Either both or none of these move messages should be dispatched. If it is only possible to dispatch one of the move messages, the widget may get "stuck" at the shared position and thereby block other cross-robot movements.
- *Collision avoidance.* We want to avoid collisions at the shared position; at most one widget can occupy the shared position at any point in time.
- *Sequencing.* During a cross-robot movement, the first robot must release the shared widget before the second robot can grab it.

In the following, I demonstrate how synchronizers allow the programmer to express the group-level integrity requirements directly.

The first requirement states that with a cross-robot movement, either both or none of the move messages should be dispatched. We can enforce this requirement with an atomicity constraint that ensures indivisible dispatch of move messages sent by the top-level object. This atomicity constraint should apply only to move messages that are part of cross-robot movement.

The second requirement avoids collisions at the shared position. We can avoid collisions at the shared position by insisting that at most one cross-robot movement is under way at any time. If one of the robots dispatches a move message associated with one cross-robot movement, we can avoid collisions by preventing the other robot from dispatching a move message associated with another cross-robot movement. The synchronization constraints at robots ensure that each robot executes only one move operation at a time. Moreover, the atomicity constraint that ensures dispatch of either both or none of the move messages also ensures that both robots execute move operations associated with the same cross-robot movement. Hence, the combination of the atomicity constraint that addresses integrity requirement number one and the synchronization constraints at individual robots ensure that at most one cross-robot movement is under way at any time.

The third requirement states that the first robot must release before the second robot can grab. This constraint can be enforced by a combination of triggers and disabling constraints that order the dispatch of `release` and `grab` messages.

Although the sharing of widgets requires coordination between the two robots, it is desirable if the robots can operate asynchronously except for cross-robot movement. If it receives a move request that involves only a single object, the top-level object delegates the move request without any constraints attached. The absence of constraints for single-robot move requests ensures asynchronous operation except for cross-robot movement.

Whenever the top-level object initiates a cross-robot movement, it also instantiates a synchronizer that enforces the coordination required for that particular cross-robot movement. Thus, there is a one-to-one correspondence between instantiated synchronizers and cross-robot movements.

To coordinate a cross-robot movement, the top-level object instantiates a synchronizer from the template shown in figure 3.11. Each synchronizer instantiated from the `robots` synchronizer template coordinates a specific cross-robot movement; the parameters of the `robots` template identify a specific cross-robot movement. The name `passer` refers to the robot that passes a widget in a specific cross-robot movement, and the name `receiver` refers to the robot that receives a widget in a specific cross-robot movement. The `receiverHand` parameter is the hand component of `receiver`. The names `start` and `end` are bound to the start and end destinations, respectively; the name `shared` identifies the position that is shared between the robots. The instantiated synchronizer must know these three positions in order to constrain the correct messages.

The relations defined in the `robots` synchronizer template enforce the necessary coordination for cross-robot movement. The atomicity constraint ensures that both robots are involved in the same cross-robot movement at the same time. The atomicity constraint also ensures that at most one widget is positioned in the shared area at any time. The disabling constraints and triggers enforce the necessary temporal ordering between the actions taken by the two robots. In terms of temporal ordering, the integrity requirements of the composed robots state that the passing robot must place the widget at the shared position before the re-

```
synchronizer robots(passer,receiver,receiverHand,start,
                    end,shared)
    passerActive := false;

  atomic
    (passer.move(from,to) if from = start  and to = shared,
     receiver.move(from,to) if from = shared  and to = end);
  disable
    receiverHand.grab if passerActive;
  trigger
    passer.move(from,to) if from = start  and to = shared
       → { passerActive := true; };
    passer.releaseDone → { passerActive := false; };
end robots;
```

Figure 3.11
A synchronizer that coordinates cross-robot movement

ceiving object can grab it. Furthermore, the passing robot must release the widget before the receiving robot can start moving it. Synchronizers instantiated from the **robots** template implement the temporal ordering requirement by disabling the **grab** method in the receiving hand until the passing robot is done releasing. Because a robot does not start moving a widget until it has grabbed the widget, preventing the grab operation also prevents the move operation.

The **passerActive** instance variable helps ensure that the **grab** method in the receiving hand is not disabled until the passing robot has initiated its **move** operation. We do not want to disable the grab method while other **move** requests are being served by the receiving robot. The variable **passerActive** indicates whether the passing robot has initiated its **move** operation. □

The robot example illustrates some of the issues involved in constructing a hierarchy of concurrent objects. The top-level object delegates messages to the two robots. Because the robots are subject to group-level integrity requirements, they must dispatch the delegated messages in a certain order. For example, the robots must dispatch the **move** messages delegated as part of a cross-robot movement as an atomic action. However, since the robots have synchronization constraints, they may delay and reorder delegated messages, and the order in which messages are dispatched by the robots may be different from the order in which they are delegated by the top-level object. Thus, the top-level object cannot maintain the group-level integrity requirements simply by delegating messages in a certain order; the top-level object needs to use additional mechanisms, such as synchronizers, in order to maintain group-level integrity.

Without synchronizers, the top-level object and the robots would have to exchange control communication to ensure that messages are dispatched in accordance with the group-level integrity requirements. However, exchange of control communication requires that we change the robots and include methods for control communication in their interface. Thus, without synchronizers, we cannot reuse the existing robots. With synchronizers, the top-level object can enforce the group-level integrity requirements without changing the robots. Since the group-level integrity requirements are enforced transparently, we can reuse the same kind of robot as part of different hierarchies with different integrity requirements.

Besides reuse, synchronizers also provide modularity. It is possible to change the behavior of the robots, including their synchronization constraints, without changing the coordination enforced by synchronizers. For example, I defined two kinds of robots in example 3: `Robot` and `ObstacleRobot`. Instances of `Robot` implement the basic robot behavior, whereas instances of `ObstacleRobot` can operate in an environment with physical obstacles. In example 7, I introduced the `robots` synchronizer as a means to coordinate two instances of `Robot`. However, I could, without modification, use the `robots` synchronizer to coordinate two instances of `ObstacleRobot`.

Another advantage of modularity is that it is possible to enforce a different synchronizer without changing the behavior of the coordinated robots. For example, it is possible to enforce a synchronizer that causes the passing robot not to release a shared widget until the receiving robot has grabbed the widget. This synchronizer would be necessary if widgets could not be put down in the shared position.

Example 8 Multimedia Synchronization

Consider a multimedia system with an output device for audio (e.g., a loudspeaker) and an output device for video (e.g., a video monitor). A video server sends a stream of video frames to the video device, and an audio server sends a stream of digitized sound samples to the audio device. I illustrated the structure of this kind of multimedia system in figure 1.2.

We can model the multimedia system as a collection of distributed objects and express communication between servers and devices in terms of message passing. For example, the video server sends messages to the video device. Each of these messages contains a video frame.

There is a logical relationship between video frames and audio samples: certain samples "belong" to certain frames. This relationship gives rise to an integrity requirement for the object group (i.e., for the video device and the audio device): the two devices must dispatch messages in an order that maintains the relationship between video frames and audio frames. It is not necessary to dispatch messages in a lock-step manner; it is sufficient that the two devices dispatch messages within a certain tolerance.

We assume that the multimedia system has a *session* concept. A session could be a video clip with associated audio explanations. The servers initiate a session by sending a `start` message to the devices. The `start` message resets the devices. The video device has a `display` method that dispatches messages with video frames. The `display` method takes a video frame as parameter and displays this frame. Similarly, the audio device has a `play` method that plays audio samples.

Both devices have access to a local clock in order to produce output in the real-time rate required, such as 25 video frames per second. The video device records the time at which frames are shown on the monitor. When `display` is invoked, the current time is compared to the previous recorded time. If the difference is less than the required rate, the object suspends itself for the difference. If the difference is greater than the required rate, the frame is shown right away. A similar scheme is implemented in the audio device.

Video frames and sound samples are tagged with a sequence counter that allows the output devices to process input in sequence and discard "old" input. This ordering can be described by synchronization constraints at the devices. It should be noted that these synchronization

```
synchronizer lipSynch(audio,video,tolerance)
    numAudio := 0;
    numVideo := 0;

  trigger
    audio.start → { numAudio := 0; };
    video.start → { numVideo := 0; };
    audio.display → { numAudio := numAudio + 1; };
    video.display → { numVideo := numVideo + 1; };
  disable
    audio.display if numVideo - tolerance > numAudio;
    video.display if numAudio - tolerance > numVideo;
end lipSynch;
```

Figure 3.12
A synchronizer that coordinates multimedia devices

constraints will delay rather than discard old input. As mentioned in section 2.2, it is possible to extend the constraint model to incorporate pattern-based deletion of messages.

The synchronizer in figure 3.12 can be used to keep the two output devices synchronized within a given tolerance. The variable numAudio keeps track of the number of played sound samples. Similarly, the variable numVideo keeps track of displayed video frames. For simplicity we assume that the output rate is the same for the two devices. The parameter tolerance denotes the maximally acceptable lack of synchronization. □

I have intentionally kept the multimedia scenario simple. However, it is possible to extend the scenario:

- Initially, the sound could be delayed until at least the first video frame has been displayed.

- The two streams do not have to start at the same time; for example, the sound could be initiated later, after displaying a certain number of frames.

By using synchronizers, multimedia streams can be synchronized without changing the involved devices. An arbitrary number of streams can be synchronized in different ways. For example, it would be possible to synchronize audio and video with the display of graphics by adding another synchronizer or by extending the above synchronizer.

Example 9 Virtual Reality
The following example is adopted from [Gib91, PBGdM93]. Consider a virtual reality system in which a virtual world is presented to a user through a head-mounted stereo display. The virtual world is created by overlaying a video stream with 3D graphics. The 3D graphics create the "contours" and surfaces of the virtual world. By moving his head, the user can focus on different parts of this virtual world.

The virtual reality system can be described as a set of distributed objects. The head device sends position measurements to a model object at a certain rate. Given a position, the model object computes a scene description for two rendering objects—one for each eye. The rendering objects generate 3D images from scene descriptions. The images are loaded into frame buffers and finally overlaid with the video frames. The system structure is depicted in figure 3.13. The head, model, and render objects constitute a pipeline. The render objects and the head device should operate at the same rate. With current technology, the render objects are the bottlenecks of the pipeline.

The virtual reality system is subject to two integrity requirements:

- The two images displayed on the stereo display must be synchronized. This synchronization can be accomplished by a scheme similar to the synchronization of multimedia streams described in example 8.
- Head movements should be synchronized with the displayed image. For example, if the model or render objects cannot keep up with the input from the head-mounted device, the rate of input from the device must be decreased temporarily. Otherwise the displayed image may suffer from a permanent lag in real time. Decreasing the rate of measurements at the head device will appear as temporary slow motion, which is assumed to be better than a permanent delay.

Suppose the head-mounted device has a `measurePosition` method that measures the current position and sends the result to the model. The device has a clock so that measurements can be done in real time.

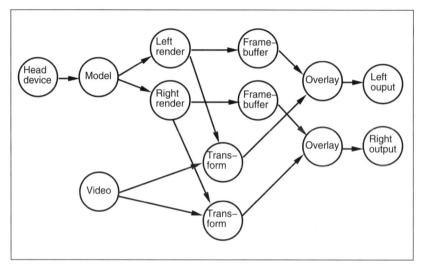

Figure 3.13
Structure of a virtual reality system

Similar to the output devices in example 8, the head device records the previous measurement time. When invoked, the `measurePosition` method may have to suspend for a certain amount of time before it actually performs the position measurement.

```
synchronizer adjustRate(head,render,tolerance)
    pipeline := 0;

  trigger
    render.nextScene → { pipeline := pipeline - 1; };
    head.measurePosition → { pipeline := pipeline + 1; };
  disable
    head.measurePosition if pipeline > tolerance;
end adjustRate;
```

Figure 3.14
A synchronizer that adjusts the rate of position measurements

Render objects have a `nextScene` method that is invoked by the model with the next scene description. The synchronizer in figure 3.14 keeps track of the number of active elements in the pipeline for one of the render objects. If the size of the pipeline exceeds a certain threshold, the rate of measurements at the head device is slowed by the temporarily disabling invocation of the `measurePosition` method. The synchronizer in figure 3.14 must be instantiated twice—once for each render object.
□

Using synchronizers to describe the virtual reality system gives considerable flexibility. The integrity requirements can be implemented in different ways without changing the objects of the system. For example, if the head device was implemented purely in hardware, it may not be possible to slow its measurement rate. If the head device's measurement rate cannot be slowed, we need to discard certain measurements instead. Measurements can be discarded by a synchronizer that prevents dispatch of "old" measurements. By discarding old measurements, the model can jump past a certain time segment and thereby allow the render objects to process measurements that are current.

It should be emphasized that the examples are not comprehensive; synchronizers are applicable in number of other application domains.

3.7   Possible Extensions

Since the main goal for the language constructs is to motivate and demonstrate the applicability of synchronizers, I focused on simplicity when designing the constructs. However, the constructs can be extended in many ways to increase their expressiveness. The following sections describe and discuss such possible extensions. All of the proposed extensions could be integrated with the current set of language constructs without interference.

3.7.1   Constraining Specific Messages

Since the constructs are based on pattern matching, a synchronizer applies to messages based on their structural properties such as destination and content. However, in some cases we want to distinguish between messages with the same structure and constrain only a subset of them.

The robot example (example 7) illustrates a scenario where we want to draw a finer distinction between messages than directly supported by pattern matching. The `robots` synchronizer is instantiated for each pair of `move` messages that constitutes a cross-robot movement. There is a one-to-one correspondence between synchronizers and message pairs, and each synchronizer should restrict only a specific message pair. When using pattern matching to define the scope of synchronizers, we need to construct patterns that match only a specific pair of `move` messages. In order to construct such patterns, we are forced to parameterize the synchronizer explicitly with values that correspond to the content of messages. This explicit parameterization is inelegant. A more desirable solution directly associates synchronizers with message pairs.

A possible extension is to enable the definition of synchronizers that apply only to messages sent within a given block of code. Transactions are typically specified in this manner: the root of a transaction is typically defined as all messages sent within a "transaction block."

Implementation of explicit binding between synchronizers and messages is not complicated. Messages could be tagged by the implementation so that they contain information about the block of code from which they were sent. If a synchronizer S is bound to a block B, the implementation could ensure that S's patterns match messages only with B's tag. It is more elegant and efficient to perform the tagging at the implementation level rather than at the language level, thus hiding tags from the programmer.

3.7.2   Conditions for Synchronizer Enforcement

With the constructs, having a reference to an object is a necessary and sufficient condition for enforcing a synchronizer on that object. However, it is possible to employ other models of constraint enforcement. For example, objects could be required to possess certain capabilities in order to enforce constraints on other objects. Such authorization checking would strengthen the conditions for synchronizer enforcement. Another approach would be to weaken these conditions and make it possible for objects to enforce synchronizers on other objects based on their type or other attributes.

The appropriate conditions for synchronizer enforcement depend on the host language and the specific application of synchronizers within that language. By changing the semantics of pattern matching, the constructs can be extended to include different kinds of conditions for synchronizer enforcement.

3.7.3   Multimessage Patterns

An atomicity constraint consists of n patterns, but it is not possible to describe relations between the parameters of these patterns. For example, it is not possible to express an atomicity constraint that can be satisfied only by a message set where all messages in the set have the same content. In order to describe such relations, we would extend the notion of pattern to match multiple rather than single messages.

Consider the following tentative syntax for multimessage patterns:

a.m(x) × b.n(y) if x = y

In this pattern, a and b are objects and m and n are methods in these objects. The intention is for the pattern to be matched by a set of two messages, one for a and one for b, where the two messages have the same content. The expression of the pattern could be any expression over x and y.

Multimessage patterns are relevant only for the description of atomicity constraints where multiple messages are dispatched as one logical action. If messages are dispatched one at a time, the functionality of multimessage patterns can be simulated by multiple single-message patterns that share the same state.

Although multimessage patterns may increase the expressive power of the model, I have decided to keep the model as simple as possible and not include them. Note that the model does not prevent inclusion of multimessage patterns.

3.7.4   Incremental Strengthening of Atomic Constraints

With our constructs it is not possible to instantiate a synchronizer that "strengthens" the atomicity constraints in other synchronizers. Consider the dining philosophers problem in example 6. In the example, the indivisiblePickup synchronizer enforces indivisible pickup of two chopsticks. But suppose that we want to refine the scenario so that philosophers also need a spoon in order to eat. In this refined scenario, we want to enforce an atomicity constraint that provides indivisible pickup of two chopsticks *and* a spoon. We cannot describe this refined scenario by instantiating another synchronizer to supplement the indivisiblePickup synchronizer.

```
synchronizer refined(c1,c2,spoon,phil)
  atomic
    (c1.pickup(p1) if p1 = phil,
     c2.pickup(p2) if p2 = phil,
     spoon.pickup(p3) if p3 = phil);
end refined;
```

Figure 3.15
A synchronizer that enforces indivisible access to two chopsticks and a spoon

Suppose that we instantiate the **refined** synchronizer in figure 3.15 along with the **indivisiblePickup** synchronizer described in figure 3.7. If the two chopsticks **c1** and **c2** each received a **pickup** message from the philosopher **phil**, the atomicity constraint in the **indivisiblePickup** synchronizer would be satisfied, regardless of the atomicity constraint in the **refined** synchronizer, and it would be possible for **phil** to pick up his chopsticks without picking up a spoon.

With the constructs, the only way to strengthen an atomicity constraint is through textual editing. If we want to enforce indivisible pickup of two chopsticks *and* a spoon, we would have to add a pattern explicitly for spoon pickup to the **indivisiblePickup** synchronizer.

One approach that supports incremental strengthening would be to name atomicity constraints and provide an operation that strengthens a named constraint. For example, suppose the atomicity constraint in the **indivisiblePickup** synchronizer has the name **chopstickPickup**. Then we can imagine a constraint of the form:

strengthen chopstickPickup **with**
  (spoon.pickup(p3) **if** p3 = phil)

With this incremental operation, philosophers would now be forced to pick up a spoon along with their chopsticks. In order to keep the constructs as simple as possible, I have not included this kind of incremental modification. Once again, there is nothing that prevents its inclusion.

3.8   Related Work

Related work can be divided into a number of categories. These include
transactions, atomic broadcasting, synchronous multiparty interactions,
and graph rewriting. We examine these alternative approaches to group-
level coordination after looking at a commonly used ad hoc approach:
an explicit coordinator.

3.8.1   Explicit Coordinators

In conventional languages, an explicit *coordinator* object often maintains
the integrity requirements of a group of objects by regulating access to
the group. Clients of the object group access the group through the
coordinator, not directly. The coordinator delegates client messages to
the group and coordinates the group by delegating these messages in a
certain order. The resulting system structure is sketched in figure 3.16.

Although a coordinator is a separate entity, it cannot transparently
coordinate a group of objects that each has its own synchronization constraints. The coordinator coordinates a group of objects by delegating
messages to them in a certain order. However, if the group members
have synchronization constraints, delegated messages may be delayed
and reordered at these objects, and the coordinator cannot assume that
messages are dispatched in the same order that they were delegated.
Thus, in order to ensure the group's integrity, the coordinator needs
to exchange control communication with the objects in the group. Exchange of this control communication is not transparent to the objects.

Even if we were willing to sacrifice transparency, explicit coordinators
still have drawbacks compared to synchronizers:

- A coordinator is a potential bottleneck since it centralizes all communication to the object group. In contrast, a synchronizer may be
  implemented in either a centralized or distributed manner. Moreover,
  even if a synchronizer has a centralized implementation, it will centralize those messages only that it constrains.

- The control communication exchanged between a coordinator and an
  object group is explicit. With synchronizers, this control communication is part of the underlying implementation. Using explicit control
  communication increases complexity at the language level and hard-
  wires the implementation of group-level coordination into the objects.

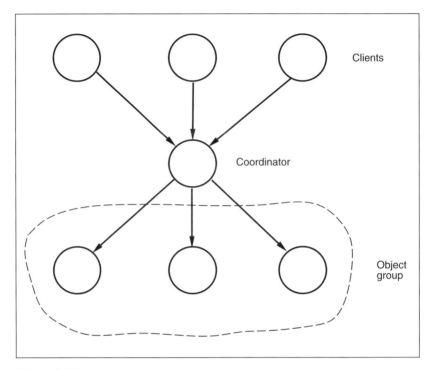

Figure 3.16
An explicit coordinator

For example, if the coordinator must ensure atomic dispatch of messages, a commit protocol would have to be hard-wired into the participating objects. With synchronizers, the commit protocol is part of the implementation. If the control communication is part of the implementation, it is possible to adapt the commit protocol to the underlying systems architecture without changing the program.

- Coordinators cannot overlap. Suppose we want to enforce two distinct coordination schemes on the same group of objects. With explicit coordinators, we need to specify one coordinator that enforces both schemes. With synchronizers, we can define two separate synchronizers and compose them. The ability to compose synchronizers promotes modularity.

3.8.2   Transactions

Transaction systems [LS82, WL88, DHW88, KHPW90, GCLR92, WY91] offer a notion of atomicity. In these systems, atomicity is defined as serializable mutation of *state*. In contrast, our notion of atomicity is concerned with the dispatch of messages and thereby with the initiation of activities. Our atomicity constraints specify indivisible dispatch of messages at multiple objects. Since activities are initiated by the dispatch of messages, indivisible dispatch also ensures indivisible initiation of activities at multiple objects.

In many systems, integrity or correctness is based on activities rather than state. For example, this is the case in many process control systems such as the system illustrated in the robot example (example 7). In the robot example, integrity was defined in terms of the activities that robots carry out (move, grab, and release), not the state of robots. With atomicity constraints, we can specify that a cross-robot movement requires that both robots initiate a "move" activity. We could not express this requirement in terms of traditional transactions over the state of robots.

3.8.3   Atomic Broadcast

A number of systems provide broadcasts with atomic delivery guarantees. Examples include ISIS [BJ87], Consul [MPS91], and the notion of interface group proposed in [OOW91]. These systems are based on the notion of object (or process) group, and they provide a means to send an atomic broadcast to a group. An atomic broadcast is typically guaranteed to be delivered to all nonfailed members of a group. Moreover, delivery of a broadcast is an indivisible action; the delivery of one broadcast is not interleaved with the delivery of other broadcasts. All objects that receive the same two broadcasts receive them in the same order.

These systems guarantee only indivisible delivery of messages, they do not guarantee that delivered message are dispatched as an indivisible action. An object's synchronization constraints may delay and reorder delivered messages and thereby undermine the notion of atomicity guaranteed by the broadcast system. In contrast, synchronization constraints cannot undermine the message-ordering constraints implemented by synchronizers. Synchronization constraints and synchronizer constraints are evaluated as an atomic action.

Another drawback of atomic broadcast systems is that messages are ordered according to a built-in criterion: the indivisible delivery of broadcasts. In many applications, the integrity of object groups requires message ordering according to user-defined criteria. That was the case, for example, in the multimedia system described in example 8. In the multimedia system, messages had to be ordered within a user-defined tolerance. Another problem with using a built-in criterion is that all messages to a group are ordered. With synchronizers, it is possible to order the dispatch of specific messages; message dispatch is not ordered unless explicitly specified by the programmer.

3.8.4 Multiparty Interactions

Languages with synchronous communication, such as CSP [Hoa78], provide a notion of atomicity. In these languages, a communication consists of an input event at the receiver and an output event at the sender. The input event and output event associated with a given communication occur as one atomic action.

Multiparty interaction languages [ESFG88, FHT86, EFK89, JS91, AFL90, BKS88, Cha87] generalize this notion of atomicity so that an atomic communication can involve multiple output events and a single input event. A number of senders communicate with a shared receiver, and this communication is an atomic action. The receiver specifies a template for possible interactions; it specifies the number of participants and possibly a list of properties that individual participants must satisfy. Participants then refer to this template in order to "enroll" in the interaction specified by the template.

In multiparty interaction languages, coordination is specified as an integral part of the objects (or processes) themselves. In contrast, our approach is to separate objects from coordination in order to provide transparency and modularity. Furthermore, multiparty interaction languages do not provide a way to specify temporal ordering of messages.

3.8.5 Triggers

A notion of triggering is supported in Procol [vdBL91]. Triggers in Procol are called *propagator constraints*. Suppose we have two line objects, `line1` and `line2`, each with a `draw` method that draws the line. Consider the following propagator constraint:

constraint `line1.draw()` → { `line2.draw()` }

This propagator constraint ensures that whenever an object sends `draw` to `line1`, a `draw` message is automatically sent to `line2` (by the run-time system). In contrast to synchronizers, propagators are regular statements, which means that they are specified inside objects. Moreover, propagators can only *generate* messages; they cannot prevent or delay the dispatch of messages.

The Tahiti language [HJ90] contains events as first-class objects. In terms of triggering, Tahiti introduces a special **whenever** clause that executes a block of code whenever a specified event occurs. The occurrence of events in one process can be observed by other processes through a **reveal** clause. As in Procol, the triggers in Tahiti can only observe, not constrain, the occurrence of events.

3.8.6 Multimedia Synchronization

Several languages and libraries have been constructed in order to describe the synchronization present in multimedia systems e.g., [Ste90, BHL91]. These languages are tailored for the area of multimedia synchronization. In contrast, our notion of synchronizer provides a general model for the description of multiobject synchronization. Besides this high-level distinction between our approach and languages for multimedia synchronization, there are also differences in the technology used. In the following, I compare the constructs to one of the more sophisticated and flexible proposals for multimedia synchronization.

In [Gib91], an object-oriented framework is presented for the connection and synchronization of multimedia objects. The notion of "composite" multimedia object is central to the framework. A composite multimedia object has a number of parts that are primitive multimedia objects. A composite multimedia object can synchronize its parts.

For example, we could use the multimedia framework to describe the multimedia system in example 8. Using the multimedia framework, we could describe the multimedia system as two primitive multimedia objects, `audioSink` and `videoSink`, and a composite multimedia object, say, `audioVideo`, that has `audioSink` and `videoSink` as parts. The objects `videoSink` and `audioSink` correspond to the devices in exam-

ple 8. The role of the object `audioVideo` is to synchronize `audioSink`
and `videoSink`. It would do so by explicit communication with these
objects. For example, the `audioVideo` object would periodically invoke
control methods in the `audioSink` and `videoSink` objects to monitor
their rate of progress. If `audioSink` lags behind, the `audioVideo` object
would invoke a control method in `videoSink` to slow the display rate.

In comparison with synchronizers, the framework in [Gib91] achieves
synchronization by corrective actions such as slowing the display rate.
Use of such corrective actions for synchronization assumes that it is
possible to compensate for integrity violations rather than avoid them.
Although this may be possible in multimedia systems, it is not possible in
general. For example, compensation would not be possible in example 7
where we used synchronizers to maintain the integrity of a group of two
robots. In the robot example, a synchronizer prevented collisions at a
shared position that could be reached by both robots. It would not be
possible for the implementation to compensate for a collision that results
in damage to one or more widgets.

Another important difference between synchronizers and the multimedia framework is that the multimedia framework requires exchange
of explicitly programmed control messages, which makes coordination
nontransparent.

3.8.7 Constraint-Based Languages

Constraint-based languages such as [Ste80, Lel88] allow declarative specification of relations between variables. Furthermore, the run-time system maintains the relations by propagating updates. For example, consider the relation $x = y$. If the value of x is changed, the implementation
will automatically apply the same change to y.

The Kaleidoscope language [FBB92] supports constraints in an object-
oriented setting. Constraints in Kaleidoscope support the specification
of relations between a group of objects. Although the actual constraints
are specified separately from the constrained objects, the constrained
objects must explicitly provide an implementation for the imposed constraints. For example, if two graphical objects `g1` and `g2` were subject
to the constraint `g1.position = g2.position`, these objects would have
to implement the = constraint in terms of their representation. Moreover, objects in Kaleidoscope are sequential, and there is no notion of
temporal ordering or atomicity.

3.8.8 Global Assertions

In [CR82, Ray88], synchronization is described as global assertions for a distributed system. Cast in terms of objects, an assertion is an expression over the instance variables of a group of distributed objects. If updating a variable will violate the assertion, the update is delayed. If it later becomes possible to update the variable without violating the assertion, the update is allowed to proceed at that time.

As an example, suppose we want to express exclusive access to a shared resource in terms of a global assertion. Each object that accesses the resource would then have a variable v_i, and there would be an assertion of the form $v_1 + \ldots + v_n \leq 1$. Before accessing the resource, an object would attempt to increment its variable v_i, and after use an object would decrement its variable. The increment operation would block until no other object is accessing the shared resource, and an object is allowed to proceed only when all the v_i's are 0. The decrement operation would never block; it would allow other objects to access the resource.

Since a global assertion is specified in terms of the instance variables of objects, it exposes these instance variables and thereby violates encapsulation. Furthermore, global assertions provide no way of describing atomicity.

3.8.9 Graph Rewriting

Graph rewriting is used to specify concurrent systems in [KLG93]. A concurrent system is represented as a graph, and the execution of a system is given by a set of productions that rewrite the graph. Certain productions represent the dispatch of messages at objects. Productions can have a guard associated with them, making it possible to describe conditional dispatch of messages. Furthermore, because a production can rewrite multiple objects as an atomic action, the formalism provides a notion of indivisible dispatch of messages.

Although productions can be guarded, the associated conditions cannot be history sensitive without violating encapsulation: guards can refer to the state of objects but do not have a state of their own. In contrast, a synchronizer has its own state and does not depend on the state of the constrained objects.

3.8.10   Documentation of Coordination

Several approaches document, rather than implement, group-level coordination at an abstract level. In [Ara91], a temporal logic framework is used for capturing the message-passing behavior of objects.

The notion of a *contract* is proposed in [HHG90, Hol92]. Contracts extend object types to capture the message-passing obligations that must be fulfilled by objects.

In [Isl95], a mix of path expressions, data flow, and control flow is used to express the design constraints of a subsystem. Expressing these constraints directly makes it easier for programmers to construct customized subsystems.

The above proposals describe rather than prescribe group-level coordination. The expression of coordination serves to document and verify the way in which objects interact. The proposals do not provide an implementation of the expressed coordination. In contrast to these proposals, synchronizers are "executable specifications" of coordination.

3.9   Conclusion

Synchronizers support the description of message-ordering constraints for a group of objects. In describing such constraints, we find that the following properties are essential:

- *Logical separation.* Synchronizers are specified as distinct entities; ordering constraints are *not* part of objects. This physical separation between objects and synchronizers provides separation of design concerns. One design concern is the behavior of objects; that is, the algorithms performed in response to messages. Another design concern is the relative timing of algorithm execution in different objects; that is, *when* algorithms may be executed. Separating these two design concerns makes it easier, and less prone to error, to construct and maintain a distributed application.

- *Transparency.* Synchronizers are specified in a manner that is transparent to the specification of objects. Because synchronizers are transparent, they can be used to construct distributed applications from reusable objects; the same object can be used in different contexts with different ordering constraints enforced by different synchronizers.

- *Interfaces as boundaries*. The functionality of synchronizers is specified in terms of the interactions between objects rather than their internal representation. First, this means that synchronizers do not expose the internal representation of objects, and thereby violate encapsulation. Second, the same synchronizer can be applied to different object groups if they interact in the same way. This creates a potential for synchronizer reuse.

Synchronizers express the necessary coordination of an object group as part of the context of objects, not as part of the objects themselves. Besides facilitating reuse, describing interobject coordination external to objects also captures an important property of real-world objects: the behavior of objects may be constrained by their context.

Synchronization constraints and synchronizers both provide message-ordering constraints. Synchronization constraints order only the messages received by a single object; synchronizers order the messages received by multiple objects in a group. Uniformity has been a specific design goal: it is desirable if both kinds of ordering constraints can be described using the same fundamental principles. We achieve this uniformity by describing both kinds of constraints in terms of message patterns.

It is important that a language supports both synchronization constraints and synchronizers. If a language supports only one of these concepts, it is complicated and error prone for the programmer to implement the other in an ad hoc manner. The primary source for this complication is that the language implementation of one construct and the ad hoc implementation of the other construct must work together to provide atomic evaluation.

4 Semantics

To provide a formal definition of synchronizer semantics, I define a simple programming language that contains synchronizers and distributed objects and give an operational semantics for this language. The language is designed to capture the essential concepts of synchronizers and distributed objects; it is not designed to express these entities as efficiently or elegantly as possible.

The language is based on the Actor model of concurrent computation, and the semantics of the language extends the semantics described in [AMST96, AMST92]. However, there are some differences. For example, in traditional Actor languages, messages are always guaranteed to be dispatched eventually by their destination actor. In our language, we need a generalized notion of message dispatch—a notion where message dispatch is subject to synchronizers.

4.1 Language Overview

I define a simple language, called LOS (language with objects and synchronizers), that captures the essence of distributed objects and synchronizers. Unlike most programming languages, LOS is not intended to be expressive and provide ease of programming. Instead, LOS is designed so that its semantics will provide a clear and elegant definition of synchronizer semantics. A goal in LOS's design is to keep nonsynchronizer constructs to a minimum so as not to complicate or clutter the semantics unnecessarily. I have therefore ignored general object-oriented concepts such as encapsulation, typing, and inheritance. The semantics of these concepts has been addressed elsewhere (e.g., in [Car84, CW84, Coo89, PS94]), and the semantics of synchronizers is orthogonal to the semantics of these concepts.

I do not include explicit constructs for synchronization constraints in LOS. Synchronization constraints are operationally equivalent to single-object synchronizers: they both constrain the dispatch of messages by a single object. As explained in section 3.2, describing synchronization constraints by single-object synchronizers either violates encapsulation or leads to unnecessary double bookkeeping. Although separating synchronization constraints and synchronizers is an important concern from a programming and software engineering point of view, from an operational and semantic point of view there is no need to distinguish between them.

The LOS language supports the Actor model of distributed and concurrent computation [Agh86]. Hence, distributed objects are captured by *actors*. Each actor has a unique *address*, which is its location-independent identity. Actors communicate only by message passing, and in order to send a message to an actor, its address must be known by the sender. Since addresses are first-class values that may be communicated in messages, the communication topology is dynamic. Message passing is asynchronous, and message delivery is guaranteed to happen eventually.

Although message delivery is guaranteed, synchronizers may prevent an actor from actually dispatching a delivered message. Hence, I distinguish strongly between message *delivery* and message *dispatch* in LOS. When the communication subsystem places a message in an actor's input queue, the message has been delivered. Message dispatch occurs when the actor starts to process the message.

Actors are reactive entities that perform activities only in response to messages. The activity performed by an actor is prescribed by its *behavior*. An actor's behavior is a closure [Lan64]: a procedure and an environment in which the procedure is executed. In LOS, behaviors are described as lambda abstractions in an untyped, call-by-value lambda calculus.

A message has two parts: an address, which specifies the receiver of the message, and a value, which constitutes the content of the message. When an actor dispatches a message, it applies its behavior, a lambda abstraction, to the value part of the message. Note that the content of a message is exactly *one* value. The communication of complex data can be achieved by sending a composite value.

Traditional lambda abstractions are purely functional. However, it is important to be able to describe actors whose behavior depends on their past invocation history. For example, we would like to be able to define a bank account actor whose current behavior depends on the dispatch of past deposit and withdrawal messages. In order to capture this kind of *history sensitivity*, the Actor model introduces the notion of *replacement behavior* for an actor. In response to a message, an actor's lambda abstraction computes the abstraction to be applied to the next message. This next abstraction is called the actor's replacement behavior. With replacement behaviors, an actor has an associated *sequence* of behaviors—one behavior for each message that it has dispatched. Notice that an abstraction does not have to specify a different abstraction as replacement behavior: it can specify itself as replacement behavior.

The concept of replacement behavior captures state mutation, which is a fundamental concept in object-oriented programming. An actor's behavior is its state, and this state can be changed by means of behavior replacement. Without behavior replacement, actors would be functional entities.

The notion of replacement behavior is just one extension to the basic lambda calculus that LOS introduces. In general, LOS extends the lambda calculus with the following commands for actor creation, message passing, and synchronizer instantiation:

- **send** for sending a message.

- **become** for specifying a replacement behavior. The argument passed to **become** is the lambda abstraction to be applied to the next message.

- **newadr** for allocating a new actor address. The result of executing **newadr** is a "fresh" actor address.

- **initbeh** for initializing a newly allocated actor. The **initbeh** command takes two arguments: a newly allocated actor address and the lambda abstraction to be used as the initial behavior of that actor.

- **enforce** for instantiating a synchronizer. The argument of **enforce** is a synchronizer to be instantiated.

These commands are modeled as primitive functions in the lambda calculus.

Rather than have one command for actor creation, LOS distinguishes between allocation of a new actor's address (**newadr**) and initialization of a new actor's behavior (**initbeh**). This distinction is made in order to facilitate the definition of actors that initially know their own address and to facilitate the definition of multiple actors that initially know each other's address.

An actor a that wants to create an actor b first calls **newadr** in order to allocate the address of b. Then a calls **initbeh** in order to provide the initial behavior for b. After its address has been allocated, b cannot receive messages until it has been initialized with a behavior. Moreover, only a can initialize the behavior of b.

Synchronizers neither send nor receive messages. Instead, a synchronizer *observes* and *constrains* the dispatch of messages by actors. Because of this fundamental difference between synchronizers and actors, we do not model synchronizers as actors. Instead, we incorporate a notion of synchronizer as a primitive language construct in LOS.

There is no notion of method in LOS; the behavior of an actor has only one procedure. The concept of method is not fundamental from an operational standpoint: we can simulate the functionality of methods by explicitly communicating values that serve as method "identifiers."

4.2   Language Syntax

In this section, I provide a formal definition of LOS's syntax. In defining LOS's syntax, I assume a countable set of variables Var and atoms Atom. Variables are placeholders for values. The set Atom contains primitive values such as integers, Booleans, and `nil`.

Furthermore, we assume the existence of a set Op_n that contains the primitive operations of rank n. A distinction is made between two kinds of primitive operations: primitive functions Fun and primitive commands Com. Primitive functions are side-effect free maps, such as `not` and `pr`. Primitive functions map values to values. Primitive commands provide the actor primitives, such as `send` and `become`. Primitive commands may have side effects in the sense that their execution may affect other actors.

The primitive functions of rank n are in Fun_n, and the primitive commands of rank n are in Com_n. The set Op_n is the set of primitive operations with rank n and is the union of Fun_n and Com_n. Finally, the set Op is the set of all primitive operations regardless of rank.

$x \in \mathsf{Var}$

$a \in \mathsf{Atom} = \{\texttt{true}, \texttt{false}, \texttt{nil}, 0, 1, \ldots\}$

$\mathsf{Fun} = \cup_{n \in \mathsf{Nat}} \mathsf{Fun}_n = \{\texttt{first}, \texttt{second}, \texttt{not}, \texttt{pr}, \texttt{branch}, \ldots\}$

$\mathsf{Com} = \cup_{n \in \mathsf{Nat}} \mathsf{Com}_n = \{\texttt{newadr}, \texttt{initbeh}, \texttt{send}, \texttt{become}, \texttt{enforce}\}$

$f_n \in \mathsf{Op}_n = \mathsf{Fun}_n \cup \mathsf{Com}_n$

$f \in \mathsf{Op} = \cup_{n \in \mathsf{Nat}} \mathsf{Op}_n$

The set Nat includes all the natural numbers $1, 2, 3, \ldots$ and 0.

$$
\begin{aligned}
e \quad &::= \quad v \\
&\mid \quad e_1\, e_2 \\
&\mid \quad f_n(e_1, \ldots, e_n) \\
v \quad &::= \quad a \\
&\mid \quad x \\
&\mid \quad s \\
&\mid \quad \lambda x.e \\
&\mid \quad \texttt{pr}(v_1, v_2) \\
s \quad &::= \quad \texttt{synch}(r) \\
r \quad &::= \quad r_1;\, r_2 \\
&\mid \quad \texttt{atomic}(p_1, \ldots, p_n) \\
&\mid \quad \texttt{disable}(p) \\
&\mid \quad \texttt{trigger}(p, e) \\
p \quad &::= \quad e_1(x)\,\texttt{if}\, e_2
\end{aligned}
$$

Figure 4.1
Abstract syntax for LOS

The syntax involves five categories: expressions ($e \in$ Exp), irreducible values ($v \in$ Value $\subseteq$ Exp), synchronizers ($s \in$ Synch $\subseteq$ Value), relations ($r \in$ Relation), and patterns ($p \in$ Pattern). A relation can be either a constraint or a trigger. The abstract syntax for LOS is given in figure 4.1.

The syntax contains "standard" elements from the lambda calculus [Bar84] such as definition and application of lambda abstractions. A lambda abstraction "$\lambda x.e$" has a formal parameter, x, and a body, e. An abstraction's formal parameter is a variable, and an abstraction's body is an expression. Application is the only operation on abstractions. Application is written as juxtaposition; for example, the expression "$(\lambda x.e)\, v$" applies the abstraction "$\lambda x.e$" to the value v. Informally, applying an abstraction to a value v involves evaluating the abstraction's body in an environment where the abstraction's formal parameter is bound to v. The general form of application is $e_1\, e_2$ where the expression e_1 must evaluate to an abstraction, and the expression e_2 may evaluate to any value.

In the remainder of this section, we examine the description of primitive operations, actors, and synchronizers in LOS. Section 4.2.4 introduces example actors and synchronizers described in LOS.

4.2.1 Primitive Operations

The primitive **pr** function is a constructor for pair values. A pair is a composite value with two components that each can be arbitrary values. For example, the expression **pr**$(3+4, 5+3)$ evaluates to a pair value with 7 as the first component and 8 as the second component. In general, the components of a pair can again be pairs, allowing for construction of arbitrarily complex information structures.

The functions **first** and **second** are the only extractors defined on pair values. The first component of a pair is returned by **first**, and the second component of a pair is returned by **second**. It should be noted that a pair of values such as **pr**$(4, \texttt{nil})$ can be considered an expression as well as a value. This ambiguity is resolved by the convention that pairs of values are themselves values.

The primitive function **branch** has rank 3 and captures branching. Intuitively, the functionality of **branch** is as follows. First, the arguments are evaluated. If the first argument evaluates to **true**, the value of the second argument is returned. If the first argument does not evaluate to **true**, the value of third argument is returned.

Unlike "if" statements in traditional programming languages, **branch** evaluates all its arguments. However, based on **branch**, we can define an **if** function that evaluates its arguments conditionally:

$$\texttt{if}(e_0, e_1, e_2) = (\texttt{branch}(e_0, \lambda z.e_1, \lambda z.e_2)) \texttt{ nil}$$

The second and third arguments of **if** are not evaluated until a choice, based on the first argument, has been made. This delayed evaluation is accomplished by wrapping the second and third argument in a closure. In the definition of **if**, it is required that the variable z does not occur free in e_1 or e_2.

4.2.2 Actors

Traditionally, variables are placeholders for values, but here variables also represent actor addresses. Rather than introduce a special set of actor addresses, we model them as elements of Var. We can then capture the concept of actor address without extending LOS with special-purpose constructs. Treating actor addresses as elements of Var ensures that they are first-class values that can be communicated in messages.

The behavior of an actor is described as a lambda abstraction. Representing actor addresses by variables implies that an actor's behavior may contain "unbound" variables, namely, the variables that represent the addresses of other actors.

4.2.3 Synchronizers

The behavior of a synchronizer is given by a synchronizer value. Synchronizer values are constructed by the **synch** operator. Synchronizer values are first-class values so that we can abstract over them by normal lambda abstraction. If synchronizer values were not first-class values, we would have to include special constructs to express parameterized synchronizers.

A synchronizer value is a structured entity that consists of a number of relations. A relation can be either a constraint or a trigger. In LOS, there are two kinds of constraints—**disable** and **atomic**—and one kind of trigger—**trigger**. Relations are meaningful only within the context of a synchronizer. It is not necessary to pass relations as parameters or bind them to variables. Hence, relations do not need to be first-class values.

As in chapter 3, patterns are the basic building blocks of relations. A pattern "$e_1(x)$ if e_2" has three parts: a *destination* e_1 that identifies an actor, a *parameter* x that is bound to the content of messages, and a *body* e_2 that is evaluated during pattern matching. The destination of a pattern evaluates to the address of an actor. A pattern matches a message sent to its destination if the body e_2 evaluates to **true** in a context where x is bound to the content of the message. In LOS, patterns have only one parameter because messages always have exactly one value as content.

The notion of state mutation is similar for synchronizers and actors. In both cases, state mutation is described by behavior replacement. Recall that the behavior of an actor is given by a lambda abstraction, and behavior replacement is described by the **become** command. The behavior of a synchronizer is given by a synchronizer value, and behavior replacement is described by triggers.

A trigger consists of a pattern and a body. A trigger's body is an expression. Whenever an actor dispatches a message that matches a trigger's pattern, the trigger's body expression is evaluated. If the body evaluates to a synchronizer value, this synchronizer value is the replacement behavior for the enclosing synchronizer. If the body does not evaluate to a synchronizer value, the enclosing synchronizer remains unchanged.

The behavior of a synchronizer can be history sensitive in the same manner as an actor behavior. A synchronizer has a sequence of behaviors; a replacement behavior is computed whenever a trigger, in the synchronizer, evaluates its body. Moreover, a replacement behavior is the *result* of evaluating the body of a trigger. Since a trigger's body can refer to its enclosing synchronizer, behavior $i + 1$ of a synchronizer can depend on behavior i.

The body of a trigger cannot have side effects. In LOS, the only expressions with side effects are the actor commands such as **become** and **send**. In evaluating the body of a trigger, such commands are not evaluated. The body of a trigger is evaluated by a functional evaluation relation that does not evaluate actor commands. This relation treats actor commands as irreducible entities. If a trigger's body contains actor commands, that trigger will never install a replacement synchronizer. A replacement is installed only if the body evaluates to a synchronizer value; otherwise the enclosing synchronizer remains unchanged.

4.2.4   Examples

In this section I show the definition of example actors and synchronizers in LOS. Although the syntax is less verbose than the syntax introduced in chapter 3, the underlying principles are the same. In particular, LOS does not ignore any significant operational aspects of the constructs introduced in that chapter.

In practice, it is often the case that synchronizers and actors replace themselves with the same behavior in a different binding environment. This gives rise to self-referential, or recursive, behaviors. I illustrate the issues of recursion in LOS through a simple example: a recursive factorial function.

One of the more direct ways to specify a recursive factorial function **fact** is to write a circular definition:

```
fact = λn.if(n = 0,1,n * (fact (n - 1)))
```

Here, "=" is a primitive equality operation, and "−" and "*" are primitive arithmetic functions with their usual interpretations. But the above definition of fact is not a priori a meaningful LOS definition; LOS does not provide a notion of circular definition. We need a way to define recursive structures in LOS without using circular definitions.

As an alternative to circular definitions, I describe recursive structures as least fixed points of functionals. For example, the least fixed point of the following LOS functional is a recursive factorial function:

```
λf.λn.if(n = 0,1,n * (f (n - 1)))
```

This functional is a meaningful LOS expression. However, for functionals to be a practical way to define recursive structures, we need a way to compute the least fixed point of functionals within LOS. Since LOS is untyped, we can define, within LOS, a *recursion operator* [MT91] rec, that computes the least fixed point of functionals. The constructs of LOS do not present any complications with respect to recursion, and rec can be a conventional call-by-value fixed-point combinator such as the rec_v operator defined in [MT91]. Rather than give a formal definition of rec, I will illustrate its use. For example, rec can be used to define a recursive factorial function, fact, in LOS as follows:

```
fact = rec λf.λn.if(n = 0,1,n * (f (n - 1)))
```

The variable f is called a *recursion variable* because references to f represent self-reference.

In the following, I use rec to define recursive actor and synchronizer behaviors. For example, consider the definition of LOS expressions in figure 4.2. The expression sink defines the (recursive) behavior of an actor that ignores its messages. Assume that an actor a has the sink behavior. When a receives a message, the name m is bound to the value of this message. After receiving a message, a "becomes" the same behavior, which in this case is the sink behavior. The variable b is a recursion variable that allows the sink behavior to refer to itself.

The expression takeTurns defines a (recursive) function that returns a synchronizer value. The takeTurns function illustrates parameterization of synchronizers in LOS. Instead of introducing a special parameter

```
sink = rec λb.λm.become(b)

takeTurns = rec λme.λturn.
  synch(
    disable(x(z) if turn = y)
    trigger(y(z) if true,(me x))
    disable(y(z) if turn = x)
    trigger(x(z) if true,(me y))
  )


manager = λz.enforce(takeTurns x)
```

Figure 4.2
Example actors and synchronizers in LOS

mechanism for synchronizers, I use traditional lambda abstraction to describe parameterization of synchronizers. A parameterized synchronizer is described by "wrapping" a synchronizer value in a lambda abstraction. The parameter of the lambda abstraction represents the synchronizer parameter. For example, the parameter **turn** of the **takeTurns** abstraction represents a synchronizer parameter. The body of the lambda abstraction is a synchronizer value that describes the behavior of the parameterized synchronizer.

The synchronizer value inside the **takeTurns** abstraction defines four relations: two constraints and two triggers. The variables x and y represent actor addresses, and they are therefore not bound by the **takeTurns** abstraction. The relations capture an ordering constraint under which the actors with address x and y take turns dispatching messages. At any point in time, the variable **turn** is bound to the name of the actor who may currently dispatch a message.

The first disabling constraint prevents the actor x from dispatching messages if **turn** is bound to y. Notice that the pattern of this disabling constraint declares a "dummy" variable z whose value is not used in the body of the pattern. The need to declare this dummy variable is dictated by the syntax for patterns—patterns *must* declare a variable. Requiring that all patterns declare exactly one variable is not very elegant but immaterial from a semantic standpoint.

The first trigger in the **takeTurns** abstraction replaces the current synchronizer value with another synchronizer value when y dispatches a message. The replacement synchronizer value is equal to the current synchronizer value except for the binding context: **turn** is bound to x in the binding context of the replacement synchronizer value. The variable **me** is a recursion variable. The application of **me** to the variable x yields a synchronizer value that constitutes the replacement behavior.

The second disable constraint and trigger have a functionality that is similar to the first disable constraint and trigger, except that the constraint applies to x instead of y, and the trigger applies to y instead of x. There is no way, in LOS, to capture this similarity in structure. We could do this with a construct such as "**for** ... **in**" as introduced in chapter 3. However, such a construct is not essential for our notion of synchronizer, so one is not included in LOS.

The **manager** abstraction in figure 4.2 defines the behavior of an actor that instantiates the synchronizer represented by the **takeTurns** abstraction. The **manager** abstraction instantiates a synchronizer in a way that gives the initial turn to the actor with address x. As in the **takeTurns** abstraction, the variable x represents an actor address and is therefore unbound. The variable z is a dummy variable.

4.3   Representation of Actor Systems

A *configuration* is a symbolic instantaneous representation of an actor system with respect to some idealized observer [Agh86]. I specify a transition relation between configurations. One configuration C_1 is related to another configuration C_2, under the transition relation, if C_2 can be the result of executing a single primitive action in configuration C_1. The transition relation plays the role of "interpreter" for actor systems because it specifies the result of executing primitive actions.

In the semantics, I model concurrency between actions as the potential for arbitrary interleaving of these actions. A transition corresponds to a primitive action such as sending a message or performing a single step in the evaluation of an expression. Multiple transitions may be possible from a given configuration. For example, a configuration may contain multiple actors that are all "ready" to perform an action. I want to model the fact that, in a distributed system, these actors may execute their actions concurrently. I model concurrency by specifying in the semantics that the choice between multiple transitions from the same configuration is nondeterministic. With a nondeterministic choice, any interleaving of the corresponding actions is possible.

In describing the semantics, I use the following notation for sets and maps. $P_\omega[X]$ is the set of finite subsets of X. $M_\omega[X]$ is the set of finite multisets with elements in X. The set of maps from X to Y is denoted $I_{map}[X, Y]$, and $F_{map}[X, Y]$ is the set of finite maps from X to Y. The operator $\uplus$ denotes multiset union, and "M, m" is shorthand for $M \uplus \{m\}$. The cardinality of a (multi)set M is specified as $\#M$.

4.3.1   Representation of Actors

Creating an actor involves two operations: one to allocate the actor's address and another to initialize the actor's behavior. After it has been created, an actor is either waiting for a message, or it is evaluating its behavior in response to a message. To capture this life cycle of an actor, we say that an actor can be in one of three *modes*: uninitialized, waiting, or busy.

An actor is in the uninitialized mode from the time its address is allocated until its behavior is initialized. The mode of an uninitialized actor whose address was allocated by another actor x is denoted $(?x)$. The mode of an uninitialized actor contains information about its creator (in this case, the creator is x). Because the mode of an uninitialized actor contains information about the actor's creator, it is possible to ensure that only the actor's creator is able to initialize the actor's behavior.

An actor is waiting if it is ready to process a message. The mode of a waiting actor is denoted (v), where v is the actor's current behavior. v is the behavior that will be evaluated in response to the next message.

A busy actor is currently evaluating its behavior in response to a message. If e is the expression currently being evaluated by a busy actor, the mode of that actor is denoted $[e]$.

The set of possible actor modes is referred to as **Mode**. With the syntax for actor modes introduced in the previous paragraphs, elements mo of **Mode** have the following structure:

$$mo ::= (?x) \mid (v) \mid [e]$$

An actor map α is a finite map that, given an actor address, returns the mode of that actor. An actor map allows us to determine the mode of an actor if we know its address. Actor maps have the following domain and range:

$$\alpha \in \mathrm{F}_{map}[\mathsf{Var}, \mathsf{Mode}]$$

Recall that we represent actor addresses as elements of Var.

An actor map that maps the actor x to the mode mo is denoted mo_x. The "," operator defines composition of actor maps. For example, the actor map "$\alpha, (v)_x$" has domain $\mathsf{Dom}(\alpha) \cup \{x\}$ and maps x' to $\alpha(x')$ if $x' \neq x$ and maps x to (v).

4.3.2 Representation of Messages

Actors communicate by message passing. A message is a structured entity that consists of an actor address (the destination of the message) and a value (the content of the message). However, not all values can be communicated in messages. In the following I explain which values are *communicable values*.

Because the body of a lambda abstraction may contain **become** commands, we do not allow lambda abstractions to be communicated in messages. If an actor x sends a lambda abstraction with a **become** command to an actor y, and if y evaluates this abstraction, the **become** command would change the behavior of x because LOS has static scoping. We do not want one actor to cause behavior replacement at another actor, and we prohibit communication of lambda abstractions.

A communicable value is any value except lambda abstractions. The set CValue defines the set of communicable values, and the set $\mathsf{Message}$ is the set of messages that can be sent by actors. The following rules define the structure of CValue and $\mathsf{Message}$:

$$cv \in \mathsf{CValue}$$

$$m \in \mathsf{Message}$$

$$cv ::= a \mid x \mid s \mid \mathbf{pr}(cv_1, cv_2)$$

$$m ::= \langle x \Leftarrow cv \rangle$$

4.3.3   Configurations

Given the above definitions of actors and messages, we can now formally define the notion of configuration. A configuration is a three tuple consisting of an actor map, a multiset of messages, and a set of synchronizers. The actor map gives the mode of each actor in the system. A configuration contains a multiset of messages rather than a set of messages. With a message set, two messages with identical values sent to the same actor would be modeled as only one element. The synchronizers of a configuration observe and constrain the dispatch of messages by actors.

The set of configurations is called Configuration. Elements of this set have the following structure:

$$\alpha \in \mathrm{F}_{map}[\mathsf{Var}, \mathsf{ActorState}]$$
$$\mu \in \mathrm{M}_{\omega}[\mathsf{Message}]$$
$$\sigma \in \mathrm{P}_{\omega}[\mathsf{Synch}]$$
$$\kappa \in \mathsf{Configuration}$$
$$\kappa ::= \left\langle\, \alpha \mid \mu \mid \sigma \,\right\rangle$$

A configuration's actor map must be total, that is, the map's domain must contain all the configuration's free variables. In order to express this totality requirement, we need to define formally a function FV that returns a LOS term's free variables. The inductive definition of FV is given in figure 4.3.

As can be observed from figure 4.3, variables are bound only by lambda abstraction and pattern definition. A variable bound by a lambda abstraction is visible in the abstraction's body; a variable bound by a pattern is visible in the pattern's body. Moreover, a variable that is bound by a trigger's pattern is visible in the trigger's body.

Given the definition of FV, it is possible to define the free variables of actor modes. The function FV_{mo} returns the free variables of an actor mode:

$$\mathrm{FV}_{mo}((?x)) = \{x\}$$
$$\mathrm{FV}_{mo}((v)) = \mathrm{FV}(v)$$
$$\mathrm{FV}_{mo}([e]) = \mathrm{FV}(e)$$

$$
\begin{aligned}
\mathrm{FV}(a) &= \emptyset \\
\mathrm{FV}(x) &= \{x\} \\
\mathrm{FV}(\lambda x.e) &= \mathrm{FV}(e)\backslash\{x\} \\
\mathrm{FV}(\mathtt{pr}(v_1, v_2)) &= \mathrm{FV}(v_1) \cup \mathrm{FV}(v_2) \\
\mathrm{FV}(\mathtt{synch}(r)) &= \mathrm{FV}(r) \\
\mathrm{FV}(e_1\ e_2) &= \mathrm{FV}(e_1) \cup \mathrm{FV}(e_2) \\
\mathrm{FV}(f_n(e_1, \ldots, e_n)) &= \mathrm{FV}(e_1) \cup \ldots \cup \mathrm{FV}(e_n) \\
\mathrm{FV}(r_1; r_2) &= \mathrm{FV}(r_1) \cup \mathrm{FV}(r_2) \\
\mathrm{FV}(\mathtt{atomic}(p_1, \ldots, p_n)) &= \mathrm{FV}(p_1) \cup \ldots \cup \mathrm{FV}(p_n) \\
\mathrm{FV}(\mathtt{disable}(p)) &= \mathrm{FV}(p) \\
\mathrm{FV}(\mathtt{trigger}(e_1(x)\,\mathtt{if}\,e_2, e_3)) &= \mathrm{FV}(e_1) \cup ((\mathrm{FV}(e_2) \cup \mathrm{FV}(e_3))\backslash\{x\}) \\
\mathrm{FV}(e_1(x)\,\mathtt{if}\,e_2) &= \mathrm{FV}(e_1) \cup (\mathrm{FV}(e_2)\backslash\{x\})
\end{aligned}
$$

Figure 4.3
Definition of free variables

We can now formally express the fact that actor maps are total functions. Let α be the actor map of a configuration with message set μ and synchronizer set σ. If $A = \mathsf{Dom}(\alpha)$, then α must satisfy the following rules:

1. If $x \in A$ then $\mathrm{FV}_{mo}(\alpha(x)) \subseteq A$.

2. If $\langle x \Leftarrow cv \rangle \in \mu$ then $\mathrm{FV}_{mo}(cv) \cup \{x\} \subseteq A$.

3. If $s \in \sigma$ then $\mathrm{FV}(s) \subseteq A$.

Although actor maps must be total, individual actors may contain free variables. A closure that represents the behavior of an actor may have free variables, namely, the variables that denote the addresses of other actors.

As I have previously mentioned, a configuration is a snapshot of an actor system. It represents an actor system's state at a specific point in time during execution. Execution itself is modeled by a transition relation on the set of configurations: a specific configuration is related to the configurations that can be obtained by a single execution step. In order to define this transition relation, we first need to capture formally evaluation of expressions, evaluation of constraints, and evaluation of triggers. In section 4.4, I define expression evaluation. Then, in section 4.5, I introduce a formal model of constraints and their evaluation. The topic of section 4.6 is the evaluation of triggers. Finally, in section 4.7, I list the possible transitions between configurations.

4.4   Expression Evaluation

In this section I formally define the semantics of expression evaluation in LOS. I define a left-to-right, call-by-value evaluation relation on expressions in a manner similar to [Rep92, WF91, MT91].

The *substitution* of an expression for a variable is a fundamental concept in connection with expression evaluation. For example, applying a lambda abstraction to a value involves substituting all occurrences of the abstraction's variable by this value in the abstraction's body.

The rules for substitution are given in figure 4.4. The substitution of an expression e' for all free occurrences of a variable x' in the expression e is written as $e[x' \mapsto e']$. Notice that substitution is defined only for *free* variables. We distinguish between the free and bound occurrences of a variable because they denote logically distinct variables that just happen to have the same name. We do not want such incidental name clashes to influence the result of expression evaluation.

We want LOS to have static scoping. Thus, in performing the substitution $e[x' \mapsto e']$ we do not want the binding operators in e to capture free variables in e'. For example, in the substitution $(\lambda x.x')[x' \mapsto (x + 3)]$, the λ binding operator should not capture the free variable x in $x + 3$. We can avoid free variable capture by renaming the bound variables in e (α conversion). In the example, we would rename the bound occurrence of x in $\lambda x.x'$ so that x would remain free in $x + 3$.

We specify the evaluation order of LOS in the form of rules that uniquely decompose an arbitrary expression into a *redex* and an *evaluation context*. A redex is the subexpression to be evaluated next. The evaluation context plays the role of "continuation," that is, the rest of the evaluation.

In LOS, a redex is the application of either a primitive function, a primitive command, or a user-defined lambda abstraction. Hence, a

$$\begin{aligned}
a[x' \mapsto e'] &= a \\
(\text{pr}(v_1, v_2))[x' \mapsto e'] &= \text{pr}(v_1[x' \mapsto e'], v_2[x' \mapsto e']) \\
x'[x' \mapsto e'] &= e' \\
x[x' \mapsto e'] &= x \\
&\quad \text{if } x \neq x' \\
(e_1\ e_2)[x' \mapsto e'] &= e_1[x' \mapsto e']\ e_2[x' \mapsto e'] \\
(\lambda x.e)[x' \mapsto e'] &= \lambda x.e[x' \mapsto e'] \\
&\quad \text{if } x \notin \text{FV}(e') \wedge x \neq x' \\
(f_n(e_1, \ldots, e_n))[x' \mapsto e'] &= f_n(e_1[x' \mapsto e'], \ldots, e_n[x' \mapsto e']) \\
(\text{synch}(r))[x' \mapsto e'] &= \text{synch}(r)[x' \mapsto e'] \\
(r_1; r_2)[x' \mapsto e'] &= r_1[x' \mapsto e']; r_2[x' \mapsto e'] \\
(\text{atomic}(p_1, \ldots, p_i))[x' \mapsto e'] &= \text{atomic}(p_1[x' \mapsto e'], \ldots, p_i[x' \mapsto e']) \\
(\text{disable}(p))[x' \mapsto e'] &= \text{disable}(p[x' \mapsto e']) \\
(\text{trigger}(p, e))[x' \mapsto e'] &= \text{trigger}(p[x' \mapsto e'], e[x' \mapsto e']) \\
(e_1(x)\ \text{if}\ e_2)[x' \mapsto e'] &= e_1[x' \mapsto e'](x)\ \text{if}\ e_2[x' \mapsto e'] \\
&\quad \text{if } x \notin \text{FV}(e') \wedge x \neq x'
\end{aligned}$$

Figure 4.4
Substitution of free variables

redex R has the following general structure:

$$R ::= (\lambda x.e)v \mid f_n(v_1, \ldots, v_n) \quad \text{where } f_n \neq \text{pr}$$

An evaluation context is an expression with a hole. The hole is denoted
□. Plugging an expression e into the hole of a context E is denoted
$E[e]$. The definition of evaluation context ensures that for all nonvalue
expressions e there exists a unique decomposition $e = E[e']$ where e' is
a redex. This decomposition points out the next step in the evaluation
of e: e' is the subexpression to be evaluated next. To obtain the desired
evaluation order, evaluation contexts E have the following format:

$$E ::= □ \mid E\ e \mid v\ E \mid f_{n+k+1}(v_1, \ldots, v_n, E, e_1, \ldots, e_k)$$

By induction on the structure of e, we could now prove that the above
definitions uniquely decompose an arbitrary nonvalue expression e into a

context E and a redex e' such that $e = E[e']$. The proof is straightforward but involves extensive case analysis of different kinds of expressions. Rather than give the proof here, I appeal to the proof sketch given in [Fel87, MT91].

Since an arbitrary expression can be decomposed into a context and a redex, I can specify the general rules for a single step evaluation of an expression by giving the evaluation rules for an arbitrary redex.

In this section, I give the evaluation rules only for redexes that are purely functional. The evaluation of actor commands, such as become, involves side effects on the configuration within which it takes place. I describe evaluation of redexes with side effects in section 4.7.

The relation $\xrightarrow{\lambda}$ reduces the functional aspect of expressions and treats actor commands as irreducible entities. The evaluation relation $\xrightarrow{\lambda}$ is the smallest relation that satisfies the following rules:

$$E[\lambda x.e \; v] \xrightarrow{\lambda} E[e[x \mapsto v]]$$

$$E[f_n(v_1, \ldots, v_n)] \xrightarrow{\lambda} E[\delta_n(f_n, v_1, \ldots, v_n)]$$

where $\delta_1, \delta_2, \ldots$ is a family of functions. The function δ_n gives the operational meaning of primitive functions with rank n:

$$\delta_n : \mathsf{Fun}_n \times \mathsf{Value}^n \to \mathsf{Value}$$

For example:

$$\delta_1(\mathtt{not}, \mathtt{true}) = \mathtt{false}$$

$$\delta_1(\mathtt{second}, \mathtt{pr}(v_1, v_2)) = v_2$$

$$\delta_3(\mathtt{branch}, v_1, v_2, v_3) = \begin{cases} v_2 & \text{if } v_1 = \mathtt{true}, \\ v_3 & \text{otherwise.} \end{cases}$$

$\vdots$

The relation $\xrightarrow{\lambda *}$ is the transitive, reflexive, and symmetric closure of $\xrightarrow{\lambda}$. If possible, the relation $\xrightarrow{\lambda *}$ reduces closed terms to canonical values. Reduction may not always be possible due to the presence of actor commands. However, if reduction is possible, the relation $\xrightarrow{\lambda *}$ is deterministic: the same term will always reduce to the same canonical value. Based on the $\xrightarrow{\lambda}$ relation, we define a partial function *eval* that given an expression returns *the* canonical value (if any) to which the term reduces.

4.5   Constraint Evaluation

In a given configuration, the dispatch of messages is subject to the configuration's synchronizers. Each synchronizer defines a number of constraints. Constraints may prevent dispatch of individual messages (**disable**) or insist that multiple messages are dispatched as one indivisible action (**atomic**).

With constraints, there are two possible ways in which messages can be dispatched:

- *Individual dispatch.* A single actor independently dispatches a message. This requires that the message does not match any pattern in a disabling constraint and an atomicity constraint.

- *Group dispatch.* A group of actors dispatch a message set as one indivisible action. For group dispatch to be possible, no message in the set must match the pattern in a disabling constraint, and the set must satisfy at least one atomicity constraint.

With both group dispatch and individual dispatch, a *set* of messages is dispatched by a *set* of actors as an atomic action. With individual dispatch, the involved set is a singleton set, and the dispatch is trivially an atomic action since only one actor is involved.

The essence of a constraint is that it either allows or prevents the dispatch of a message set. The semantics of a constraint is described as a *constraint function*. A constraint function is a Boolean predicate that maps a finite set of messages to a Boolean value. The semantics of a specific constraint is given by a constraint function that maps a message set to **false** if the constraint prevents dispatch of the message set and that maps a message set to **true** if the constraint allows dispatch of the message set.

Formally, a constraint function is a Boolean predicate that takes a finite set of messages and maps this message set to a Boolean value. The set of constraint functions is called ConFun, and this set is defined as follows:

ConFun $= \mathrm{I}_{map}[\mathrm{P}_\omega[\mathsf{Message}], \mathsf{Boolean}]$

Let cf_1 and cf_2 be two arbitrary constraint functions. The following rules define Boolean operators $\vee$, $\wedge$ and $\neg$ on the set of constraint functions:

$$(cf_1 \vee cf_2)(M) = cf_1(M) \vee cf_2(M)$$
$$(cf_1 \wedge cf_2)(M) = cf_1(M) \wedge cf_2(M)$$
$$(\neg cf)(M) = \neg cf(M)$$

These Boolean operators allow the definition of composite constraint functions. Composite constraint functions allow us to use functional decomposition in the specification of synchronizer semantics. With composition of constraint functions, we can define the semantics of a synchronizer in terms of the semantics of its constituent constraints: if we have a number of constraint functions that each represents the semantics of an individual constraint in a synchronizer, we can use the above composition operators to construct a composite constraint function that gives the semantics of the entire synchronizer. The above composition operators also allow definition of the semantics of a *set* of synchronizers in terms of the semantics of the individual synchronizers in the set.

A mapping, called C_{map}, maps an arbitrary set of synchronizers σ to a constraint function. The resulting constraint function can be applied to finite sets of messages, and it returns true for a specific message set if and only if the set can be dispatched in the context of σ. With C_{map}, we have a general way to test whether a given message set can be dispatched in a given configuration:

1. Map the configuration's synchronizers to a constraint function by means of C_{map}.

2. Apply the resulting constraint function to the given set of messages. If the result of this application is true, the message set can be dispatched; if the result is false, the message set cannot be dispatched.

The function C_{map} is defined in figure 4.5. Any message set can trivially be dispatched in a configuration without synchronizers. Hence, the function C_{map} maps an empty set of synchronizers to a constraint function *satisfied* that returns true for any message set. For a nonempty set of synchronizers, we define C_{map} in terms of three other functions D_{map}, U_{map}, and A_{map} with the same domains as C_{map}. For a set of synchronizers σ and a message set M, these functions have the following informal interpretation:

$$C_{map}, D_{map}, U_{map}, A_{map} : P_\omega[\text{Synch}] \longrightarrow \text{ConFun}$$
$$satisfied \in \text{ConFun}$$

$$C_{map}(\emptyset) = satisfied$$
$$C_{map}(\sigma) = D_{map}(\sigma) \wedge (U_{map}(\sigma) \vee A_{map}(\sigma))$$
$$satisfied(M) = \text{true}$$

Figure 4.5
The definition of C_{map}

$D_{map}(\sigma)(M) = \text{true}$ iff no message in M matches any of the patterns of disabling constraints in σ.

$U_{map}(\sigma)(M) = \text{true}$ iff no message in M matches any of the patterns of atomicity constraints in σ.

$A_{map}(\sigma)(M) = \text{true}$ iff M satisfies at least one of the atomicity constraints in σ.

The function D_{map} builds a constraint function that represents the disabling constraints of a set of synchronizers. Together the functions A_{map} and U_{map} construct a constraint function that represents the atomicity constraints of a set of synchronizers. In the following, I give the formal definition of D_{map}, A_{map}, and U_{map}.

4.5.1 Semantics of Disabling Constraints

The semantics of disabling constraints is given by the function D_{map} defined in figure 4.6. D_{map} returns a constraint function for the disabling constraints in a set of synchronizers. D_{map} is expressed in terms of the function d_{map} that returns a constraint function for the disabling constraints of an individual synchronizer. The constraint functions returned by d_{map} are composed conjunctively by D_{map}. With respect to disabling constraints, a set of synchronizers allows dispatch of a message set if each individual synchronizer allows dispatch of the message set.

An individual disabling constraint allows dispatch of a message set if the set does not contain a message that matches the constraint's pattern. Figure 4.6 specifies the semantics of individual disabling constraints us-

$$D_{map} : P_\omega[\text{Synch}] \longrightarrow \text{ConFun}$$
$$d_{map} : \text{Relation} \longrightarrow \text{ConFun}$$

$$D_{map}(\sigma \cup \{\text{synch}(r)\}) = D_{map}(\sigma) \wedge d_{map}(c)$$
$$d_{map}(r_1; r_2) = d_{map}(r_1) \wedge d_{map}(r_2)$$
$$d_{map}(\text{disable}(p)) = \neg P_{map}(p)$$
$$d_{map}(\text{atomic}(p_1, \ldots, p_n)) = d_{map}(\text{trigger}(p, e)) = \textit{satisfied}$$

Figure 4.6
The definition of D_{map}

ing the function P_{map} that maps a pattern to a constraint function. Figure 4.7 gives the definition of P_{map}. P_{map} maps a pattern to a constraint function that returns true for a message set if and only if the set contains at least one message that matches the pattern.

$$matches : (\text{Message} \times \text{Pattern}) \longrightarrow \text{Boolean}$$
$$P_{map} : \text{Pattern} \longrightarrow \text{ConFun}$$

$$matches(\langle x \Leftarrow v\rangle, e_1(x')\,\text{if}\,e_2)$$
$$= \begin{cases} \text{true} & \text{if } (eval(e_1) = x) \wedge \\ & \quad (eval(e_2[x' \mapsto v]) = \text{true}), \\ \text{false} & \text{otherwise.} \end{cases}$$

$$P_{map}(p) = f_p$$
$$\text{where}$$
$$f_p(\emptyset) = \text{false}$$
$$f_p(M \cup \{m\}) = \begin{cases} \text{true} & \text{if } matches(m, p), \\ f_p(M) & \text{otherwise.} \end{cases}$$

Figure 4.7
The definition of P_{map} and $matches$

The predicate *matches* matches a single message against a single pattern. For a message to match a pattern, the destination of the message must be the same as the address component of the pattern. Furthermore, the pattern's body expression must evaluate to `true` in a context where the pattern's variable is bound to the value of the message. The function *eval* evaluates a pattern's body expression. *eval* provides purely functional evaluation: it is free from side effects since it does not reduce actor commands.

Because expression evaluation may not always terminate, *eval* is a partial function. Thus, in writing $eval(e) = v$ we really mean: if *eval* terminates in evaluating e, the result of the evaluation is v. In practice, it is undesirable if pattern matching results in a nonterminating computation. However, nontermination is an issue only for "complex" patterns that use recursion. Moreover, non-termination can be addressed at the implementation level, where it is possible to interrupt the evaluation of a pattern body after a certain amount of time and disregard the constraint that caused nonterminating pattern matching. Since disregarding a constraint may cause dispatch of certain messages that should be blocked, a nonterminating pattern match should also result in an exception. Notice that since message passing is asynchronous and since the expression of patterns does not incur side effects, preemption of pattern matching is not directly observable by actors. At the semantic level, we want to abstract from implementation details such as preemption, and we accept the theoretical possibility of nontermination. It should be reemphasized that *eval* is deterministic: if the evaluation terminates, the result is unique.

With P_{map}, we can specify the semantics of individual disabling constraints. For an individual disabling constraint, d_{map} applies P_{map} to the constraint's pattern and negates the result by the $\neg$ constraint function operator. Hence, the constraint function returned by d_{map} for an individual disabling constraint will return `true` for a message set if and only if the message set does not contain a message that matches the constraint's pattern.

The function d_{map} is defined for all constraints and triggers. However, d_{map} "ignores" triggers and atomicity constraints by mapping them to the trivial constraint function *satisfied*. Since d_{map} conjunctively composes the constraint functions for individual constraints and triggers, *satisfied* is the "neutral" constraint function for d_{map}.

4.5.2   Semantics of Atomicity Constraints

Together, the functions U_{map} and A_{map} give a constraint function for the atomicity constraints in a set of synchronizers. There are two ways in which a message set can be dispatched in the presence of atomicity constraints: either the set is a singleton set unaffected by the atomicity constraints, *or* the set must satisfy at least one of the atomicity constraints. The functions U_{map} and A_{map} capture these two ways, respectively, and, as can be seen in figure 4.5, C_{map} composes the constraint functions returned by U_{map} and A_{map} disjunctively.

The function U_{map} is defined in figure 4.8; U_{map} returns a constraint function that determines whether a given message set is unaffected by the atomicity constraints of a set of synchronizers. The definition of U_{map} is given in terms of u_{map}, which returns a constraint function that determines whether a given message set is unaffected by the atomicity constraints in a single synchronizer.

For a message set to be unaffected by the atomicity constraints in a set of synchronizers, the message set must be unaffected by each individual synchronizer. Thus, U_{map} composes the constraint functions

---

$$U_{map} : \mathsf{P}_\omega[\mathsf{Synch}] \longrightarrow \mathsf{ConFun}$$

$$u_{map} : \mathsf{Relation} \longrightarrow \mathsf{ConFun}$$

$$card_n \in \mathsf{ConFun},\ \forall n \in \mathsf{Nat}$$

$$U_{map}(\sigma \cup \{\texttt{synch}(r)\}) = U_{map}(\sigma) \wedge u_{map}(r)$$

$$u_{map}(r_1;\, r_2) = u_{map}(r_1) \wedge u_{map}(r_2)$$

$$u_{map}(\texttt{atomic}(p_1, \ldots, p_n))$$
$$= \neg P_{map}(p_1) \wedge \ldots \wedge \neg P_{map}(p_n) \wedge card_1$$

$$u_{map}(\texttt{disable}(p)) = u_{map}(\texttt{trigger}(p, e)) = satisfied$$

$$card_n(M) = \begin{cases} \text{true} & \text{if } \#M = n, \\ \text{false} & \text{otherwise.} \end{cases}$$

Figure 4.8
The definition of U_{map}

returned by u_{map} conjunctively. A message set is unaffected by an individual atomicity constraint if no message in the set matches any pattern in the atomicity constraint. The function u_{map} captures this property by applying P_{map} to each pattern in an atomicity constraint, negating each constraint function returned by P_{map}, and conjunctively composing these negated constraint functions.

A message set with multiple elements should be dispatched as an atomic action only if it actually satisfies an atomicity constraint. Atomic dispatch of multiple messages should not happen spontaneously. In particular, dispatch of an unaffected message set should be possible only for singleton sets. This property of U_{map} is captured by the constraint function $card_1$. For all natural numbers i, $card_i$ is a constraint function that returns true for a message set if and only if the set has cardinality i.

The function A_{map} is defined in figure 4.9, and it returns a constraint function that determines whether a given message set satisfies the atom-

$$A_{map} : \mathrm{P}_\omega[\mathsf{Synch}] \longrightarrow \mathsf{ConFun}$$

$$a_{map} : \mathsf{Relation} \longrightarrow \mathsf{ConFun}$$

$$distinct,\ notsatisfied \in \mathsf{ConFun}$$

$$A_{map}(\sigma \cup \{\mathtt{synch}(r)\}) = A_{map}(\sigma) \vee a_{map}(r)$$

$$a_{map}(r_1;\ r_2) = a_{map}(r_1) \vee a_{map}(r_2)$$

$$a_{map}(\mathtt{atomic}(p_1, \ldots, p_n))$$

$$= P_{map}(p_1) \wedge \ldots \wedge P_{map}(p_n) \wedge card_n \wedge distinct$$

$$a_{map}(\mathtt{disable}(p)) = a_{map}(\mathtt{trigger}(p, e)) = notsatisfied$$

$$distinct(M) = \begin{cases} \mathsf{true} & \text{if } \forall \langle x_i \Leftarrow v_i \rangle, \langle x_j \Leftarrow v_j \rangle \in M : \\ & \quad x_i = x_j \Rightarrow i = j, \\ \mathsf{false} & \text{otherwise.} \end{cases}$$

$$notsatisfied(M) = \mathsf{false}$$

Figure 4.9
The definition of A_{map}

icity constraints in a set of synchronizers. A_{map} is defined in terms of the function a_{map} that returns a constraint function to determine satisfaction of the atomicity constraints in an individual synchronizer. Because the atomicity constraints of a set of synchronizers are satisfied if any of the atomicity constraints are satisfied, A_{map} combines the constraint functions returned by a_{map} disjunctively.

For a message set M to satisfy an individual atomicity constraint C, each pattern in C must be matched by a message in M. The set M must contain enough messages to match all the patterns in C. When applied to an atomicity constraint C, a_{map} uses P_{map} to map each pattern in C to a constraint function. The constraint functions returned by P_{map} are composed conjunctively. Conjunctive composition ensures that the resulting composite constraint function is satisfied for a message set M only if M contains enough messages to match all patterns in C. If C has a pattern that is not matched by a message in M, the constituent constraint function for this pattern returns false when evaluated on M.

A message set M with cardinality n can satisfy only an atomicity constraint with n patterns. The definition of a_{map} captures this property by conjunctively composing the constraint functions for the n patterns with $card_n$. Moreover, all messages in M must be destined for different actors. This condition is expressed in terms of the function *distinct*.

The u_{map} and a_{map} functions both ignore disabling constraints and triggers, but they ignore these entities in different ways. Because the function u_{map} uses conjunctive composition, it ignores disabling constraints and triggers by mapping them to *satisfied*. The function a_{map} uses disjunctive composition and ignores disabling constraints and triggers by mapping them to the trivial constraint function *notsatisfied*. *notsatisfied* returns false for any message set.

4.6   Trigger Evaluation

Triggers do not constrain the dispatch of messages. Instead, the triggers of a synchronizer specify possible replacement behaviors for that synchronizer. A trigger consists of a pattern and a body. When an actor dispatches a message that matches a trigger's pattern, the trigger's body is evaluated. If the evaluation yields a synchronizer value, this value gives the replacement behavior for the enclosing synchronizer.

$T_{map} : (\mathrm{P}_\omega[\mathsf{Synch}] \times \mathrm{P}_\omega[\mathsf{Message}]) \longrightarrow \mathrm{P}_\omega[\mathsf{Synch}]$

$t_{map} : (\mathsf{Relation} \times \mathrm{P}_\omega[\mathsf{Message}]) \longrightarrow \mathsf{Synch} \cup \{\mathbf{nosyn}\}$

$res : \mathsf{Message} \longrightarrow \mathsf{Pattern} \longrightarrow \mathsf{Exp} \longrightarrow \mathsf{Exp}$

$T_{map}(\emptyset, M) = \emptyset$

$T_{map}(S \cup \{\mathbf{synch}(c)\}, M)$
$$= \begin{cases} T_{map}(S, M) \cup \{\mathbf{synch}(r)\} & \text{if } t_{map}(r, M) = \mathbf{nosyn}, \\ T_{map}(S, M) \cup \{t_{map}(r, M)\} & \text{otherwise.} \end{cases}$$

$$t_{map}(r_1; r_2, M) = \begin{cases} t_{map}(r_1, M) & \text{if } t_{map}(r_1, M) \neq \mathbf{nosyn}, \\ t_{map}(r_2, M) & \text{otherwise.} \end{cases}$$

$t_{map}(\mathbf{trigger}(p, e), M \cup \{m\})$
$$= \begin{cases} res(m, p, e) & \text{if } matches(m, p)) \wedge \\ & \quad res(m, p, e) \in \mathsf{Synch}, \\ t_{map}(\mathbf{trigger}(p, e), M) & \text{otherwise.} \end{cases}$$

$t_{map}(\mathbf{trigger}(p, e), \emptyset) = \mathbf{nosyn}$

$res(\langle x \Leftarrow v \rangle, e_1(x') \text{ if } e_2, e) = eval(e[x' \mapsto v])$

$t_{map}(\mathbf{disable}(p), M) = t_{map}(\mathbf{atomic}(p_1, \ldots, p_n), M) = \mathbf{nosyn}$

Figure 4.10
The definition of T_{map}

In the semantics, we capture triggering by a function called T_{map}, which is defined in figure 4.10. The function T_{map} transforms a set of synchronizers to their replacement synchronizers. The function T_{map} takes two arguments: the set of synchronizers to be transformed and a message set, which is the set whose dispatch causes the transformation to occur. The message set passed as argument to T_{map} may be a singleton set.

The function t_{map} defines the transformation of an individual synchronizer. A synchronizer replaces its behavior if it contains a trigger that satisfies the following two conditions:

1. The dispatched message set contains a message that matches the trigger's pattern.

2. The trigger's body evaluates to a synchronizer value.

If the synchronizer does not contain a trigger that satisfies these two conditions, its behavior remains unchanged. The symbol **nosyn** is used by t_{map} to denote a situation in which a synchronizer is unchanged. If t_{map} returns **nosyn**, T_{map} simply adds the synchronizer itself to the set of transformed synchronizers. Otherwise, T_{map} adds the result of t_{map} to the set of transformed synchronizers.

The function t_{map} ignores constraints by mapping them to **nosyn**. In particular, if a synchronizer only has constraints and no triggers, its behavior will remain unchanged.

The pattern of multiple triggers in a synchronizer may be matched by the same message. If multiple triggers are matched, t_{map} chooses the first trigger encountered in the textual appearance of the synchronizer. An alternative would be to specify a nondeterministic choice between the possible triggers. However, the resulting nondeterminism is not significant from an operational point of view, and specifying a deterministic choice gives a simpler semantic model.

The function *res* evaluates a trigger's body with respect to a specific message that matches the trigger's pattern. *res* binds the trigger's variable to the content of the message, and this binding is visible to the body during evaluation. Thus, the result of evaluating a trigger's body can depend on the content of the message that caused the body evaluation to occur.

4.7   Transitions Between Configurations

With the rules for expression, constraint, and trigger evaluation, I can now define the transition relation between configurations. I define the transition relation in the form of transition rules; each transition rule specifies the behavior of a specific type of transition. Some of the transition rules are conditional; certain conditions must be met for the specific type of transition to be possible. Conditional transitions are specified using structural operational semantics as described in [Hen90, Kah88, Ast91].

$$(1) \quad \frac{\mathrm{E}[e] \xrightarrow{\lambda} \mathrm{E}[e']}{\Big\langle\, \alpha\,,\, [\mathrm{E}[e]]_x \mid \mu \mid \sigma \,\Big\rangle \xrightarrow{\kappa} \Big\langle\, \alpha\,,\, [\mathrm{E}[e']]_x \mid \mu \mid \sigma \,\Big\rangle}$$

$$(2) \quad \Big\langle\, \alpha\,,\, [\mathrm{E}[\mathtt{newadr}()]]_x \mid \mu \mid \sigma \,\Big\rangle$$
$$\xrightarrow{\kappa} \Big\langle\, \alpha\,,\, [\mathrm{E}[x']]_x\,,\, (?x)_{x'} \mid \mu \mid \sigma \,\Big\rangle \quad x'\ \text{fresh}$$

$$(3) \quad \Big\langle\, \alpha\,,\, [\mathrm{E}[\mathtt{initbeh}(x',v)]]_x\,,\, (?x)_{x'} \mid \mu \mid \sigma \,\Big\rangle$$
$$\xrightarrow{\kappa} \Big\langle\, \alpha\,,\, [\mathrm{E}[\mathtt{nil}]]_x\,,\, (v)_{x'} \mid \mu \mid \sigma \,\Big\rangle$$

$$(4) \quad \Big\langle\, \alpha\,,\, [\mathrm{E}[\mathtt{become}(v)]]_x \mid \mu \mid \sigma \,\Big\rangle$$
$$\xrightarrow{\kappa} \Big\langle\, \alpha\,,\, [\mathrm{E}[\mathtt{nil}]]_{\text{-}}\,,\, (v)_x \mid \mu \mid \sigma \,\Big\rangle$$

$$(5) \quad \Big\langle\, \alpha\,,\, [\mathrm{E}[\mathtt{send}(x',cv)]]_x \mid \mu \mid \sigma \,\Big\rangle$$
$$\xrightarrow{\kappa} \Big\langle\, \alpha\,,\, [\mathrm{E}[\mathtt{nil}]]_x \mid \mu\,,\, \langle x' \Leftarrow cv\rangle \mid \sigma \,\Big\rangle$$

$$(6) \quad \Big\langle\, \alpha\,,\, [\mathrm{E}[\mathtt{enforce}(\mathtt{synch}(r))]]_x \mid \mu \mid \sigma \,\Big\rangle$$
$$\xrightarrow{\kappa} \Big\langle\, \alpha\,,\, [\mathrm{E}[\mathtt{nil}]]_x \mid \mu \mid \sigma \cup \{\mathtt{synch}(r)\} \,\Big\rangle$$

$$(7) \quad \frac{M = \{\langle x_1 \Leftarrow cv_1\rangle, \ldots, \langle x_n \Leftarrow cv_n\rangle\} \quad (C_{map}(\sigma))(M)}{\Big\langle\, \alpha\,,\, (v_1)_{x_1}\,,\, \ldots,\, (v_n)_{x_n} \mid \mu \uplus M \mid \sigma \,\Big\rangle}$$
$$\xrightarrow{\kappa} \Big\langle\, \alpha\,,\, [v_1\ cv_1]_{x_1}\,,\, \ldots,\, [v_n\ cv_n]_{x_n} \mid \mu \mid T_{map}(\sigma, M) \,\Big\rangle$$

Figure 4.11
Possible transitions between configurations

The transition rules are given in figure 4.11. The first five transition rules are similar to the rules presented in [AMST96, AMST92]. The first transition rule is concerned with functional evaluation. If the expression e at an actor x can be reduced by the relation $\xrightarrow{\lambda}$, this reduction constitutes a transition.

The second transition rule captures the fact that the result of creating an actor x' is the address of x'. Actor addresses are elements in Var, which is the set of variables. Actors must have a unique address; hence the variable denoting the address of a newly created actor must be fresh, that is, must not have been used previously.

Actor initialization is the subject of the third transition rule. Only the creating actor can initialize the created actor. This property is ensured by recording the address of the creating actor in the state of an uninitialized actor.

The fourth transition rule captures the semantics of become commands. Once an actor executes a become command, its replacement behavior is known. Hence, the actor may start to process the next message in its input queue. An actor may concurrently execute the continuation of become and start to process the next message in its input queue. Conceptually, this concurrency is internal since it takes place at one actor. However, since the concurrent threads do not have access to a shared mutable state, we model such internal concurrency by multiple actors: when an actor executes become, an anonymous actor is created and initialized with a closure that denotes the continuation of the become command. The anonymous actor carries out the rest of the computation and may send messages, create new actors, and enforce constraints. However, the anonymous actor cannot receive messages since its address is not known to any other actor. The semantics of become gives a pipelined execution model in which multiple "incarnations" of the same actor can be executing concurrently.

The symbol "_" is used to denote a fresh actor address whose actual name we do not care about. Such addresses refer to actors not known to any other actors (anonymous actors). In a configuration there may be multiple occurrences of actors with address "_". These are distinct, and simply reflect that the choice of address is irrelevant.

The fifth transition rule describes the semantics of sending a message. The effect of sending a message is to extend the multiset of messages, μ, with another element.

The sixth transition rule shows the semantics of instantiating a synchronizer. An actor can execute an `enforce` command and thereby extend the current set of synchronizers. Notice that each synchronizer value has exactly one constraint. However, according to LOS's syntax, a constraint can itself be a list of constraints composed by ";". The grouping of constraints into synchronizer values is necessary so that a replacement behavior defined by `trigger` can replace *all* the constraints of a synchronizer.

The seventh transition rule captures dispatch of messages. With constraints, a message set can be dispatched in a configuration if the set satisfies the synchronizers in the configuration. Conditional dispatch of message sets is expressed in terms of C_{map}. Applying C_{map} to the synchronizers in a configuration yields a constraint function. The constraint function returned by C_{map} can be applied to a message set, and if the result of this application is true, the set can be dispatched. It should be noticed that even though a message set M does not satisfy a set of synchronizers, subsets or supersets of M may satisfy the synchronizers.

The transition rules define an abstract interpreter for LOS and provide an operational semantics for synchronizers. One of the important roles of the semantics is to state formally what it means for actions to be atomic. The notion of atomicity is fundamental in describing the functionality and consistency of synchronizers. The informal semantics in chapter 3 stated that the following three kinds of activities should be atomic actions:

- The activity of instantiating a synchronizer.

- The activity of dispatching a message and executing the actions triggered by dispatching this message.

- The activity of dispatching a message set that satisfies an atomicity constraint.

The atomicity of a single transition is used to model the atomicity of these activities: each activity is modeled as a single transition in the operational semantics.

4.8   Discussion

The semantic description focuses on the dynamic aspects of actors and synchronizers. I have taken a simple approach to the static semantics LOS, giving a description of the context-free structure of language terms. In particular, I did not provide a type system for LOS. With a type system it would be possible to capture additional information about the well-formedness of terms. For example, it would be possible to capture the fact that the argument passed to the become command must be a closure. The dynamic semantics merely captures the fact that the argument must be a value. Defining a type system for LOS would be possible; however, developing a type discipline would not provide new insights about constraints. Hence, I have chosen to ignore the issue of static typing.

My semantic model of constraints is not inherently tied to my specific syntactic notion of constraints. The concept of constraint function can capture many different kinds of constraints. The only aspect of constraints built into the semantic model is that constraint functions are Boolean predicates on finite sets of messages. By changing C_{map}, it is possible to incorporate different kinds of constraints. For example, it would be possible to include multimessage patterns, as introduced in section 3.7.3, by changing the definition of P_{map}. A multimessage pattern has the following form:

a.m(x) $\times$ b.n(y) if x = y,

where a and b are actors and m and n are methods in those actors. The above pattern is satisfied by two messages, one message to a and one message to b, if the two messages contain the same values. In my current definition of P_{map}, a pattern is satisfied by a message set if the set contains a message that matches the pattern. Satisfaction of a multimessage pattern would require that each element of the set "maps" uniquely to an element of the multimessage pattern and that the expression of the pattern evaluates to true under this mapping. The important thing to note is that we can include multimessage patterns and other extensions in the semantic framework without changing the fundamental concept of constraint function.

4.9   Conclusion

I have defined an operational semantics for synchronizers and objects as expressed in the "toy" language called LOS. There is a direct "mapping" from the constructs introduced in chapters 2 and 3 to corresponding constructs in LOS.

Defining the semantics of LOS has helped clarify some of the more subtle aspects of synchronizer composition, and the semantics has provided general insights about synchronizers that helped me develop the implementation described in chapter 5.

I described the semantics of concurrency as a nondeterministic choice between possible event interleavings. However, there is nothing that prevents the development of a semantics based on "true" concurrency constructs such as Petri Nets [Pet77], Event Structures [Win89], or Term Rewriting [Mes93a].

5 Implementation

I describe and discuss the principles used in the prototype implementation of synchronizers and synchronization constraints. The main goals of the implementation are to demonstrate the practicality of synchronizers and synchronization constraints and to gain further insights about the constructs. Since the implementation is a prototype, I chose to employ simple design principles rather than invest time and effort in producing a fine-tuned and highly optimized implementation. Nevertheless, the implementation is realistic and fairly efficient.

Synchronizers and synchronization constraints have been implemented as part of the BROADWAY library, a general-purpose C++ library for programming concurrent and distributed systems [Stu94]. The BROADWAY library supports the Actor model of distributed computation; it contains abstractions for defining distributed objects with their own thread of control and abstractions for describing asynchronous message-passing between objects. BROADWAY also provides a flexible meta-architecture that facilitates modular construction of placement strategies [AKP94] and dependability protocols [SA94]. I have extended the BROADWAY library with abstractions for describing synchronizers and synchronization constraints.

We examine the high-level design decisions made in constructing the implementation and identify the main issues and trade-offs involved in implementing synchronization constraints and synchronizers. I describe the implementation at several levels of detail. At the highest level, I describe the information flow between the various implementation level entities. At the most detailed level, I present pseudocode for the algorithms used in implementing synchronization constraints and synchronizers. I analyze the implementation both qualitatively (fairness and correctness) and quantitatively (performance and message complexity).

5.1 High-Level Design Decisions

We face a number of high-level trade-offs in structuring the implementation. It is important to realize that performance of an implementation is application dependent. In other words, there is not a single optimal way of implementing synchronizers and synchronization constraints. The following sections describe the most important high-level trade-offs in implementing these constructs.

5.1.1 Communication Topology

A synchronizer coordinates a distributed group of objects. At the programming language level, the coordination is transparent to the objects.
At the implementation level, however, the objects must communicate in
order to implement the coordination. There are two extreme ways of
structuring this communication: distributed and centralized. Both are
illustrated in figure 5.1. The figure describes a group of objects and a
synchronizer that coordinates the group. The shaded areas denote the
representation of the synchronizer. With a distributed communication
topology, the synchronizer's representation is fully distributed among
the objects. In order to implement the functionality of the synchronizer,
the objects must communicate directly with each other. In a centralized
communication topology, there is one shared entity that represents the
synchronizer. With a centralized topology, objects communicate with
the shared entity in order to implement the functionality of the synchronizer.

Both a distributed and a centralized communication topology have
advantages and drawbacks. A centralized topology gives rise to a single heavily shared entity that may become a bottleneck. In contrast, a
distributed topology better preserves the autonomy and asynchrony of

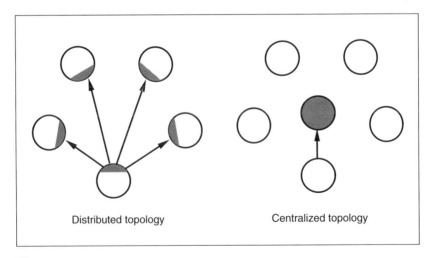

Distributed topology   Centralized topology

Figure 5.1
Distributed and centralized communication topologies

objects. However, a distributed topology may lead to excessive message traffic. Furthermore, the heuristics employed in a distributed topology may be more complicated and even inferior to the heuristics employed in a centralized system: a centralized entity has "complete" knowledge of the synchronizer and may therefore be able to make more optimal decisions. In a distributed topology no single entity has complete knowledge of the synchronizer.

In the implementation, I have chosen a hybrid solution; I centralize the representation of synchronizer state, disabling constraints, and triggers and distribute the representation of atomicity constraints. The motivation for this hybrid solution is that both disabling constraints and triggers are likely to depend on the enclosing synchronizer's state. Therefore, I want locality between disabling constraints and triggers and their enclosing synchronizer's state. On the other hand, I expect that many atomicity constraints will not depend on their enclosing synchronizer's state. If an atomicity constraint does not depend on its enclosing synchronizer's state, I would like to schedule the atomicity constraint as a fully distributed action.

5.1.2   Constraint Evaluation

In this section I use the term *constraint* to denote synchronization constraints, disabling constraints, and atomicity constraints. As in previous chapters, I say that a message *satisfies* the applicable constraints if they do not delay its dispatch, and a message is *legal* if it satisfies all applicable constraints. Constraint *evaluation* determines whether a specific message is legal.

There are two extreme implementation strategies for constraint evaluation. A *pessimistic* strategy will evaluate the constraints before dispatching a message. An *optimistic* strategy will concurrently dispatch a message and evaluate the constraints. If the constraints are not satisfied, an optimistic strategy "rolls back" the message dispatch.

Both strategies have an associated price for constraint evaluation. With a pessimistic strategy, the same price is paid whether the constraints are satisfied or not. On the other hand, an optimistic strategy pays a high price if the constraints are not satisfied and a low price if they are satisfied. Essentially the choice between a pessimistic and an optimistic evaluation strategy is governed by the expected probability of constraints being satisfied.

I have chosen a pessimistic strategy since it is less complicated to implement as part of a general-purpose library; it does not require rollback and checkpointing of object state. Moreover, since I do not want the implementation to assume a specific application domain, I cannot assume that there is a high probability that constraints are satisfied.

5.2 Synchronization Constraints

The implementation of synchronization constraints is relatively simple. There is a run-time representation of patterns, and an object's synchronization constraints are represented as a list of patterns. Checking the synchronization constraints for a message amounts to iterating through the list until either a pattern is matched or the list is exhausted. A message cannot be dispatched if it matches a pattern in the list. If, on the other hand, the list is exhausted without pattern match, the message satisfies the synchronization constraints.

We now proceed to examine the instantiation and representation of synchronizers, and we describe the evaluation of disabling and atomicity constraints defined in synchronizers.

5.3 Synchronizer Instantiation and Representation

An object instantiates a synchronizer by calling `constrain`, a library function. `constrain` does not return until the instantiation is complete; therefore, messages sent by the instantiating object after it calls `constrain` will be subject to the instantiated synchronizer.

The process of instantiating a synchronizer is illustrated in figure 5.2. An implementation level entity called a *constraint server* is created to represent the synchronizer. A synchronizer has a set of *constrained objects*—the objects that it constrains. A newly created constraint server that represents a synchronizer S notifies S's constrained objects about its existence. All the constrained objects are notified as one atomic action using a two-phase commit protocol. The notification needs to be atomic so that a system cannot be in a state where only part of a synchronizer is in effect.

During a synchronizer's instantiation, its constrained objects cannot dispatch messages that could be constrained by the synchronizer. If an

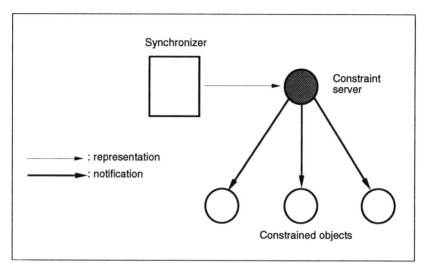

Figure 5.2
Instantiation of synchronizers

object receives a notification from a constraint server while it is executing a method, the notification message must wait for the method execution to be done: an object can execute only one method at a time.

A constraint server represents a synchronizer, and it contains the state, triggers, and disabling constraints of the synchronizer. The notification sent to objects by a constraint server contains information about the constraints and triggers at the constraint server. An object stores this information in a hash table indexed by method names. Figure 5.3 depicts the structure of this per-object *method table*. Objects add information to their method table as they are notified about instantiation of synchronizers. If an object is constrained by multiple synchronizers, its method table will contain information about the constraints and triggers in all these synchronizers. The method table contains an entry for each method that is affected by the constraints or triggers in a constraint server. Each entry contains a server list and an atomic list.

The server list contains information about the disabling constraints and triggers that apply to a given method. In particular, the server list for method m in object o contains the address of all constraint servers that enforce either a disabling constraint or trigger on "$o.m$."

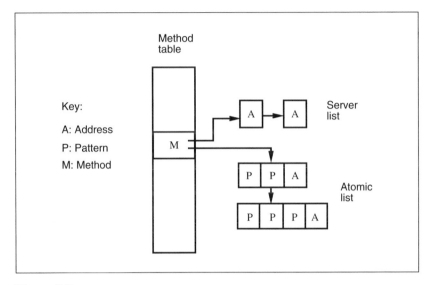

Figure 5.3
Structure of method tables

The atomic list contains information about the atomicity constraints that apply to a given method. The atomic list for method m in object o contains a representation of all the atomicity constraints that apply to the method "$o.m$." An atomicity constraint is represented by a tuple of patterns and the address of the constraint server that enforces this particular atomicity constraint. The pattern tuple represents the patterns of the atomicity constraint.

The objects and methods constrained by a constraint server remain the same throughout the lifetime of the constraint server. A trigger cannot update a pattern's object or method part; a synchronizer's patterns will match the same methods in the same objects throughout the existence of the synchronizer. Thus, a constraint server needs to notify objects only when it is created. The immutability of patterns is not dictated by the concept of synchronizers. I have chosen to have immutable patterns in order to simplify the implementation.

We do not always use distinct terminology for the implementation level entities that represent patterns, constraints, and triggers. We simply speak of "patterns," "constraints," and "triggers" when it is clear from the context whether we are referring to language-level abstractions or implementation-level representations.

5.4   Constraint and Trigger Evaluation

We now proceed to see how objects use the information stored in the method table to evaluate the applicable disabling constraints, atomicity constraints, and triggers for a given message. We do not consider evaluation of synchronization constraints; the evaluation of synchronization constraints was described in section 5.2.

Section 5.4.1 describes constraint evaluation at a high level in terms of the information flow between the involved components. Section 5.4.2 gives a more detailed picture and describes the communication protocols used to implement the information flow. An important aspect of constraint evaluation is the ability to avoid deadlocks in the evaluation protocols. Deadlock is the topic discussed in section 5.4.3.

5.4.1   Information Flow

Before dispatching a message, an object needs to check the disabling and atomicity constraints for that message. In order to check these constraints, an object finds the method table entry associated with the message.[1] If a message does not have an associated table entry, the message is not subject to any constraints. If an entry exists, the message is subject to a number of constraints.

If the server list is nonempty, the message is subject to a number of disabling constraints. These constraints are checked by querying all the constraint servers named in the server list. If all these servers respond positively, the message satisfies the applicable disabling constraints.

If the atomic list is nonempty, the message is subject to a number of atomicity constraints, and the object tries to schedule one of the atomicity constraints in the list. We say that an object schedules an atomicity constraint if it causes, or initiates, atomic dispatch of a message set that satisfies the atomicity constraint. In the implementation, atomicity constraints are symmetric in the sense that each object that is affected by an atomicity constraint may attempt to schedule the atomicity constraint.

---

1. The table lookup is dynamic because we implement constraints as part of a library. With compiler support, we could statically associate a method with its corresponding method table entry.

When an object attempts to schedule an atomicity constraint, it communicates with a number of other objects. Each element in the atomic list contains a number of patterns, and for each pattern the object sends a request to the destination object of the pattern. The object that initiates the scheduling attempt does not send a request to itself. Hence, an atomicity constraint with n patterns give rise to $n-1$ requests. Each request contains a pattern, and the receiver attempts to find a message in its input queue that matches the pattern. If a matching message is found, that message may again be subject to disabling constraints. Hence, the receiver of a request may need to query a number of constraint servers. Notice that the receiver of a request does *not* attempt to schedule any atomicity constraints: the receiver knows that an atomicity constraint for the matching message is already being scheduled. If there exists an element in the atomic list for which all $n-1$ requests can be satisfied, the message satisfies the atomicity constraints.

We speak of both messages and message sets as satisfying an atomicity constraint. Recall that a message set satisfies an atomicity constraint if each message in the set matches exactly one pattern in the constraint and all messages in the set are destined for different objects. The message sets that satisfy a given atomicity constraint are exactly those whose atomic dispatch is enabled by the constraint. We say that a single message satisfies an atomicity constraint if it is unaffected by the constraint, that is, if the message does not match any pattern in the atomicity constraint.

The patterns of an atomicity constraint may depend on the state of the enclosing synchronizer. In order to schedule such state-dependent atomicity constraints, an object must first consult the constraint server that represents the enclosing synchronizer. Because atomicity constraints are represented locally in the form of atomic lists, state-independent atomicity constraints can be scheduled using communication that involves only objects, not constraint servers.

Whenever an object dispatches a message, it notifies all constraint servers in the server list for the message so that they can execute their triggers for the message.

Figure 5.4 sketches the information flow between objects and constraint servers. Three objects, o1, o2, and o3, are subject to the synchronizer S that enforces an atomicity constraint on a messages to o1,

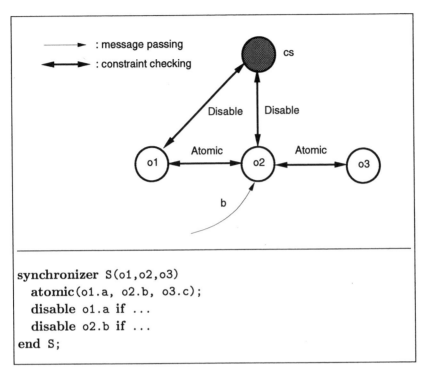

Figure 5.4
Information flow between objects and constraint servers during constraint
evaluation

b messages to o2, and c messages to o3. Furthermore, S enforces a
disabling constraint on a messages to o1 and on b messages to o2.

The constraint server cs represents the synchronizer S. The figure
illustrates the information flow when o2 evaluates the constraints for a
b message. Because b messages are subject to a disabling constraint, o2
queries cs. In order to test the atomicity constraint, o2 then sends a
request to o1 and o3. An a message at o1 satisfies this request and is
subject to a disabling constraint. Hence, o1 also queries cs in order to
check the disabling constraint for the a message.

5.4.2   Communication Protocols

The preceding section focused on the information flow in evaluating
constraints. In this section we look at the communication protocols
being used for constraint evaluation. The goal with this description is

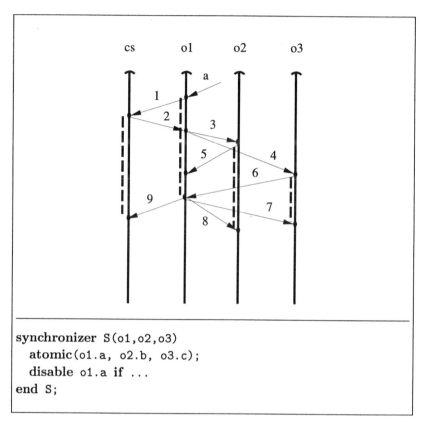

```
synchronizer S(o1,o2,o3)
  atomic(o1.a, o2.b, o3.c);
  disable o1.a if ...
end S;
```

Figure 5.5
Event diagram for constraint evaluation

to provide an intuition about the protocols based on simple examples; in section 5.5, I give a more detailed account of the protocols in the form of pseudocode.

Figure 5.5 illustrates a synchronizer enforced on three objects o1, o2, and o3. Each object has a method: o1 has method a, o2 has method b, and o3 has method c. The synchronizer enforces an atomicity constraint on all three objects and a disabling constraint on o1.

Besides the synchronizer, figure 5.5 contains an *event diagram*. A vertical line in an event diagram represents an object. Each circle on a line represents an event in the life of that object. An event corresponds to the dispatch of a message by an object. An arrow denotes message passing between objects. The starting point of an arrow is the event that caused the message to be sent, and the end point of an arrow is the event that is caused by dispatch of the message.

In the event diagram in figure 5.5, the constraint server cs represents the synchronizer S. The event diagram captures a possible history of the events involved in evaluating the constraints for a message destined for method a in object o1. Because the message is subject to a disabling constraint, o1 sends a message to cs in order to test this constraint (1). The constraint server cs determines that the message satisfies the disabling constraint and sends back a positive reply to o1 (2). Upon receipt of the reply, o1 attempts to schedule the atomicity constraint for a by sending a request to o2 and o3 (3,4). We assume that o2 has a b message in its input queue and that o3 has a c message in its input queue. Hence, both o2 and o3 send back positive replies (5,6). After receiving these positive replies, o1 knows that all constraints are satisfied. Thus, o1 dispatches the a message and informs o2 and o3 to dispatch their b and c message respectively (7,8). Finally, o1 notifies cs about the dispatch of the a message (9).

The scenario captured in figure 5.5 illustrates a *check action*, the distributed activity involved in evaluating the constraints for, and possibly dispatching, a message. A check action originates in an object called the *initiating object*. In the example, the initiating object is o1. Check actions have a *root message*—the message being checked by the initiating object. In the example, the root message is the a message received by o1.

The general structure of a check action is for the initiating object to first evaluate the disabling constraints for the root message. This evaluation requires communication with a number of constraint servers. If the root message satisfies the disabling constraints, the initiating object then evaluates the possible atomicity constraints for the root message. Evaluating an atomicity constraint with n patterns requires communication with $n - 1$ objects. These $n - 1$ objects are called *participating objects*. The initiating object sends a request with a pattern to each of the participating objects. Upon receipt of this request, a participating object examines its input queue to find a *leaf message* that matches the received pattern. In the example, the b and c messages are leaf messages. Participating objects must evaluate the disabling constraints for leaf messages. In order to check these disabling constraints, the participating objects may query a number of constraint servers.

A message set that satisfies an atomicity constraint consists of a root message and a number of leaf messages. The terms *root* and *leaf* are roles played by messages relative to a specific check action. The same message may be a root message for one check action and a leaf message for another check action.

A check action can have two outcomes: *abort* or *commit*. A check action aborts if the root message cannot be dispatched. An aborted check action has no visible effect. If a check action commits, a number of messages are dispatched at a number of objects: the root message is dispatched by the initiating object, and the leaf messages are dispatched by the participating objects. Reconsider figure 5.5. In that figure, each of the three objects o1, o2, and o3 dispatches a message as part of the same check action.

The semantics of constraints requires that check actions are atomic actions; they appear to be indivisible without any intermediate states. A check action can span multiple objects and multiple constraint servers. In order to guarantee atomicity, a check action locks all the involved entities (objects and servers) throughout its duration, until it either commits or aborts. In event diagrams, we denote a locked object by a vertical dashed line between the events that lock and unlock the object. In section 5.6, I argue that the locking scheme provides atomic check actions. Besides providing atomicity of check actions, locking also guarantees that if a check action determines that the applicable constraints are satisfied for a specific message, the constraints remain satisfied until the check action either aborts or commits.

For simplicity, check actions obtain an exclusive lock on shared entities. In an optimized implementation, it would be possible, and desirable, to distinguish between read and write locks, as well as to introduce more finely-grained locks that lock only part of an entity, such as specific instance variables in a constraint server.

In figure 5.5, only the root message was subject to disabling constraints. The event diagram in figure 5.6 illustrates a scenario in which a participating object queries a constraint server in order to evaluate the disabling constraints for a leaf message. The event diagram contains the same objects and the same synchronizer as figure 5.5. The difference between the two scenarios is that the initiating object in figure 5.6 is o2 rather than o1, and the root message is a b message. Because the b message is not constrained by disabling constraints, o2 starts by testing

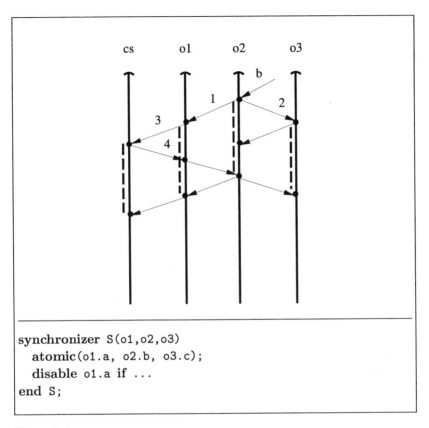

```
synchronizer S(o1,o2,o3)
  atomic(o1.a, o2.b, o3.c);
  disable o1.a if ...
end S;
```

Figure 5.6
Constraint evaluation that involves a constrained leaf message

the atomicity constraint by sending a request to the participating objects o1 and o3 (1,2). As above, we assume that both o1 and o3 have the leaf messages required by the atomicity constraint. Since a messages are constrained by a disabling constraint, o1 must first consult cs (3) before sending back a reply to o2 (4).

In the examples, messages are subject to only one atomicity constraint. If a message is subject to multiple atomicity constraints, the initiating object iterates through the atomic list for the message until the list is exhausted or a satisfied constraint is encountered. If multiple atomicity constraints are satisfied, the first one encountered in iterating over the atomic list is chosen.

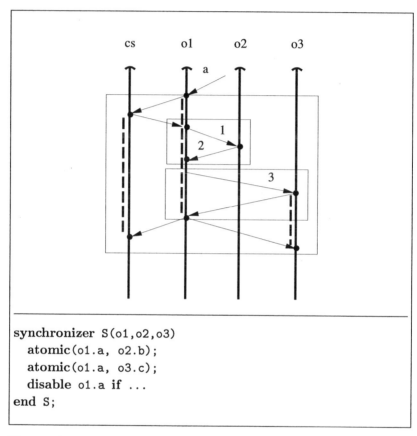

```
synchronizer S(o1,o2,o3)
  atomic(o1.a, o2.b);
  atomic(o1.a, o3.c);
  disable o1.a if ...
end S;
```

Figure 5.7
Nesting of check actions

The synchronizer S in figure 5.7 enforces two atomicity constraints on a messages. In the event diagram, o1 first attempts to schedule the "atomic(o1.a, o2.b)" constraint (1). In this example, we assume that o2 does not have a b message. Hence, the first atomicity constraint cannot be satisfied. After receiving a negative reply from o2 (2), o1 attempts to schedule the other atomicity constraint (3).

Notice that o1 retains the lock on cs while the atomicity constraints are tested one at a time. An attempt to schedule an atomicity constraint can be aborted without aborting the entire check action. In order to capture this concept, I introduce nesting of check actions. A *nested* check action can be aborted independently of its top-level check action.

Evaluating the disabling constraints for the root message is a top-level check action, and testing an atomicity constraint for the root message is a nested check action. A top-level check action can have at most one nested check action at a time: the atomicity constraints are tested one at a time. Since we do not want to abort independently the evaluation of disabling constraints for leaf messages, this evaluation does not introduce a new nesting level. Check actions have at most one level of nesting.

In figure 5.7, nesting is illustrated by containment of boxes. The box of a top-level check action contains the boxes of all the nested check actions.

A nested check action inherits the locks held by its top-level check action. A nested check action can hold locks independently of its top-level action. When a nested check action aborts, all its independently held locks are released. As illustrated, a nested check action does not release any locks also held by its top-level check action. Check actions are committed along with their top-level check actions; check actions cannot commit independently.

5.4.3   Deadlocks

The examples in section 5.4.2 are simplified scenarios in that only one check action is active at a time. In the implementation, multiple objects may concurrently initiate check actions. Because only one check action can hold the lock to an entity, we need to address the case in which a check action attempts to lock an entity that is already locked by another check action. As I illustrate, deadlocks may occur if check actions are always allowed to wait for locks held by other check actions.

Consider the event diagram in figure 5.8, and assume that check actions were always allowed to wait for locks held by other check actions. In the figure, a synchronizer enforces an atomicity constraint on two objects, o1 and o2. Both objects receive a message and initiate a check action to test the atomicity constraint. A check action always starts out by locking the initiating object. In the diagram both objects are waiting on each other; the result is a deadlock.

In the example, the deadlocked check actions wait at two objects. Deadlocks may also occur when check actions wait at constraint servers. In figure 5.9, each of two synchronizers defines a disabling constraint on

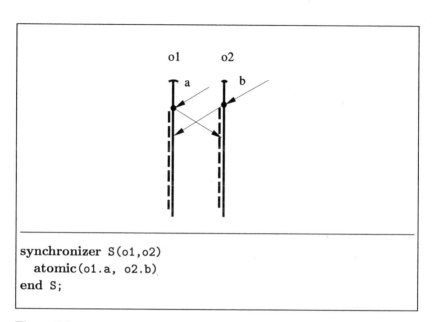

```
synchronizer S(o1,o2)
  atomic(o1.a, o2.b)
end S;
```

Figure 5.8
Deadlock between two objects

messages for both methods a and b. In the event diagram, the synchronizers are represented as two constraint servers cs1 and cs2. As above, both objects receive a message, and both objects attempt to lock both constraint servers in order to test the applicable disabling constraints. In the figure, o1 successfully locks cs1 (1) and o2 successfully locks cs2 (2). Again, both objects are deadlocked since they wait on each other.

Two check actions can also deadlock if one is waiting at an object and the other is waiting at a constraint server. The diagram in figure 5.10 shows this situation. A synchronizer S defines two atomicity constraints and one disabling constraint. The synchronizer is represented by the constraint server cs. Both o1 and o2 receive a message. The a message received by o1 is subject to a disabling constraint, and o1 sends a query to cs (1). We assume that the message is legal. After receiving a positive reply from cs (2), o1 attempts to schedule the atomicity constraint for a by sending a request to o2 (3). Concurrently, o2 attempts to schedule an atomicity constraint for b that involves c at o3 (4). We assume that o3 can satisfy the request from o2 by a c message. However, the c message

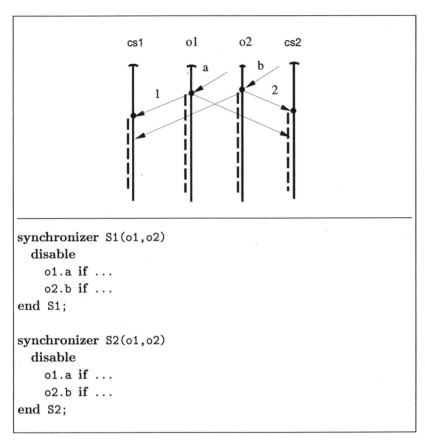

```
synchronizer S1(o1,o2)
  disable
    o1.a if ...
    o2.b if ...
end S1;

synchronizer S2(o1,o2)
  disable
    o1.a if ...
    o2.b if ...
end S2;
```

Figure 5.9
Deadlock between two constraint servers

is subject to disabling constraints, and o3 needs to query cs (5). The objects end up waiting on each other.

The three deadlock examples illustrate canonical scenarios that may lead to deadlock. In fact, the above situations capture all the possible ways in which two check actions can deadlock: at two objects, at two constraint servers, and at an object and a constraint server.

We prevent deadlocks by assigning a unique time stamp to each check action. Each check action has an associated CID (check identifier) that uniquely identifies that check action. In constructing the CID for a check action, we use the (unique) address of the initiating object. A CID is implemented as this address paired with the value of a local, per-object

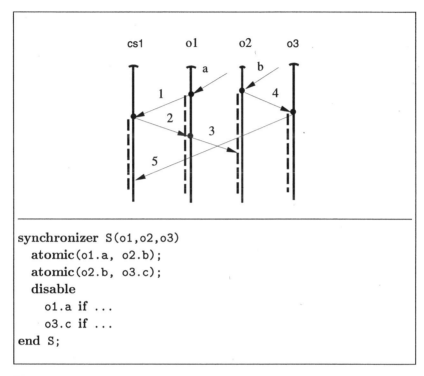

```
synchronizer S(o1,o2,o3)
  atomic(o1.a, o2.b);
  atomic(o2.b, o3.c);
  disable
    o1.a if ...
    o3.c if ...
end S;
```

Figure 5.10
Deadlock between an object and a constraint server

counter. An object's counter is incremented each time a check action initiated by the object runs to completion, without being preempted by the deadlock prevention scheme. It should be noticed that CIDs are constructed on a per-object basis in a purely distributed fashion.

We define a total order $<$ on CIDs. The $<$ order is a lexicographic order on the counter-address pairs that implement CIDs. Assume that C_1 is a CID implemented by the pair $[count_1, adr_1]$, and that C_2 is a CID implemented by the pair $[count_2, adr_2]$. Then $<$ is defined by the following rule:

$$C_1 < C_2 \quad \Leftrightarrow \quad count_1 < count_2 \text{ or } (count_1 = count_2 \text{ and } adr_1 < adr_2)$$

The order $<$ on CIDs is defined in terms of $<$ orders on counters and addresses. The $<$ order on counters is the usual "smaller than" order on integers. The counter component of a CID indicates the relative age of the CID. The $<$ order on addresses does not have a corresponding semantic interpretation; it merely serves to break ties between counters that have the same relative age. The definition of $<$ gives a total "time-stamp" order on CIDs.

We employ a wait-die deadlock prevention scheme [RSI78] based on the $<$ time-stamp order. We preempt check actions that are about to wait on a check action with a smaller (older) CID; a check action is only allowed to wait on check actions with greater (younger) CID.

If an object initiates a check action that is preempted by the deadlock prevention scheme, the object uses the same CID for its next check action. If, on the other hand, an object initiates a check action that runs to completion, the local counter is incremented and the next check action initiated by the object will have a younger CID. In this way we avoid starvation: objects that are not preempted will get relatively younger than objects that are preempted. Eventually a preempted object will have a CID old enough (relatively speaking) so that check actions initiated by the object can run to completion.

A nested check action has the same CID as its top-level check action. This facilitates lock sharing between a top-level check actions and its nested check actions; locks are held relative to CIDs.

Let us see how the wait-die deadlock prevention scheme prevents the deadlock in figure 5.8. The scenario in figure 5.11 shows how this deadlock is prevented. We assume that the counter at o1 is smaller than the counter at o2. Thus, the check action initiated by o1 is older than the check action initiated by o2. When o1's check action arrives at o2 (1), it is allowed to wait because it is older than o2's check action that currently locks o2. In contrast, when o2's check action arrives at o1 (2), it is aborted because it is younger than o1's check action that locks o1. When o2's check action is aborted, it releases the lock to o2 (3), and o1's check action can now lock o2. The other deadlock scenarios are prevented in a similar fashion.

5.5 Pseudocode

The algorithm that implements synchronizers and synchronization constraints is programmed in C++ using the BROADWAY library abstractions for concurrency and distribution. Describing the algorithm in

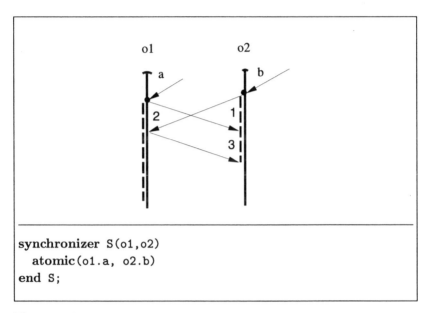

```
synchronizer S(o1,o2)
  atomic(o1.a, o2.b)
end S;
```

Figure 5.11
Deadlock between two objects

terms of high-level pseudocode allows us to abstract away from the idiosyncrasies and low-level details of C++ and BROADWAY. The pseudocode serves as a publication language and uses an Algol-like syntax to capture both the usual sequential constructs of C++ and the concurrency and distribution features of BROADWAY.

In order to capture the usual sequential constructs of C++, the pseudocode has a notion of an object that can declare instance variables and procedures to manipulate its instance variables. A pseudocode procedure is similar to a C++ function and has the usual invocation semantics. A procedure's actions are described using traditional Algol-like constructs for assignment, branching, looping, and sequencing. We use multiassignment: the notation "a,b := v,i" is a shorthand for "a := v; b := i." Procedure invocation is described using dot (".") notation: obj.proc denotes invocation of the procedure proc in the object obj. The keyword **return** returns a value to the caller of a procedure and transfers control to the caller.

In addition to the constructs that capture the usual C++ constructs, the pseudocode includes constructs that capture the BROADWAY library abstractions for concurrency and distribution. As in BROADWAY, pseudocode objects can be declared as distributed, and thereby concurrent, by means of inheritance. The class `Actor` provides the capabilities for an object to be distributed. A class that inherits from `Actor` yields instances that have their own thread of control and can be distributed. Such actor objects communicate by asynchronous message passing. The message-passing interface of an actor object consists of a number of methods. A method is similar to a procedure, except that it is invoked by asynchronous messages. Message passing can be either traditional one-way message passing, as in the Actor model, or it can be two-way request-reply style message passing. With request-reply style communication, an actor object can send multiple requests and wait for multiple replies as one logical communication. Messages are processed serially, one at a time, by an actor object, but messages are not guaranteed to be processed in the order that they were sent. We use the keyword **reply** to return a reply from a method. Returning a reply terminates the processing of a message. We introduce pseudocode notation for message passing as the need arises in describing the behavior of objects.

An actor object can declare both procedures and methods, but its procedures can only be invoked internally. An actor object can invoke methods in other actor objects by means of message passing. Furthermore, an actor object can internally declare sequential objects that serve as local data structures. An actor object can sequentially invoke procedures in such contained objects. This two-tiered object model reflects the object model provided by the BROADWAY library.

I describe the structure of a class called `ConstrainedObject` that inherits from the `Actor` class. The `ConstrainedObject` class defines the generic behavior of objects that can be constrained by synchronizers and synchronization constraints. When I talk about "objects" in this section, I refer to instances of `ConstrainedObject` or instances of subclasses derived from `ConstrainedObject`. I also describe the interface and implementation of a class called `ConstraintServer`. This is also a subclass of `Actor`. Constraint servers are instances of the `ConstraintServer` class.

Section 5.5.1 discusses the evaluation of disabling constraints. The class `ConstrainedObject` has a procedure called `checkDisable` that evaluates the disabling constraints for a given message. The topic of section 5.5.3 is evaluation of atomicity constraints. An object can play two roles in the evaluation of atomicity constraints: initiating object

and participating object. An initiating object calls the procedure called
checkAtomic. This procedure sends a number of requests to the participating objects. A participating object has a number of methods that
initiating objects call. I describe these methods and the procedure called
checkAtomic in section 5.5.3.

In section 5.5.4 I describe how an object evaluates atomicity and disabling constraints for the same message. I describe the pseudocode for a
procedure called checkMessage that evaluates the synchronization constraints and calls checkDisable and checkAtomic in order to evaluate
the disabling and atomicity constraints applicable to a given message.

Finally, in section 5.5.5, I discuss the presented pseudocode, describing the differences between the presented pseudocode and the actual
implementation.

5.5.1   Evaluating Disabling Constraints

This section describes the pseudocode for a procedure, checkDisable,
that evaluates the disabling constraints for a given message. The pseudocode for checkDisable is listed in figure 5.12. The argument m is the
message to be checked. Checking this message is part of a check action,
say CA. The arguments id and inx identify CA. The id argument is
the CID of CA. Notice that CA may be either a top-level check action or
a nested check action. As mentioned in section 5.4.3, two nested check
actions with the same top-level check action will have the same CID. If
CA is a nested check action, the inx argument provides information to
distinguish it from other nested check actions. If CA is a top-level check
action, inx has a value of 0.

The pseudocode for checkDisable illustrates the notation for asynchronous message passing. We use a "send ... to" notation for both one-
way message passing, as in "send abort(id) to servers(m)," and sending a number of requests, as in "send checkConstraints(m,id,inx)
to servers(m)." The argument of to can be either a single receiver or
a set of receivers. Waiting for replies is described by **wait for**. Below in
the pseudocode for constraint servers I introduce the notation used for
sending replies.

The procedure **servers** returns the elements of the server list for a
given message. Each element in the set returned by **servers** is the address of a constraint server, which must be queried in order to check the
disabling constraints for the message. If the set is empty, no disabling

```
procedure checkDisable(m,id,inx)
  if servers(m) = ∅ then
    return yes;
  else
    send checkConstraints(m,id,inx) to servers(m);
    wait for replies;
    if all replies are yes then
      return yes;
    if one of the replies is no then
      send abort(id,inx) to servers(m);
      return no;
    else
      send abort(id,inx) to servers(m);
      return kill;
  end checkDisable;
```

Figure 5.12
Pseudocode for `checkDisable`

constraints are currently enforced on the message, and the message trivially satisfies the disabling constraints.

The query protocol is a two-phase commit protocol. In order to check the disabling constraints for a message, an object first sends a `checkConstraints` message to each constraint server that must be queried. The response from each server can be yes, no, or kill. A yes answer indicates that the message satisfies the server's disabling constraints. A no answer indicates that the constraints are not satisfied. Finally, a kill answer implies that the check action was aborted at the constraint server as a result of the deadlock-prevention scheme: the server was already locked by another check action with an older CID.

If a query result is either no or kill, the check action is aborted by sending `abort` to all the queried servers. If, on the other hand, all the query results are yes, the disabling constraints are satisfied, and the `checkDisable` method returns yes. The method cannot by itself commit the check action because atomicity constraints may also have to be checked for the same message.

5.5.2   Constraint Servers

Figure 5.13 gives the pseudocode for constraint servers. The interface of a constraint server consists of the methods `checkConstraints`, `abort`, and `commit`. The `checkConstraints` method is called by objects in order to evaluate the disabling constraints for a specific message. The constraint evaluation takes place as part of a check action. If this check action is aborted, the object sends an `abort` message to the constraint server; if the check action is committed, the object sends a `commit` message to the constraint server.

The pseudocode in figure 5.13 introduces the notation for sending replies. Sending a reply is done by executing a **reply** statement. Reply destinations are first-class values, and the "current" reply destination is bound to the name **sender**. Having reply destinations as first-class values makes it possible to store them in data structures as regular values, and an object can defer replying to a request. Deferred replies are necessary in the description of a constraint server since requests may be stored in a request queue for later processing. Sending a reply to a specific destination is accomplished by "**reply** ... **to**," where the argument following **to** is the destination.

The pseudocode in figure 5.13 also shows that we use traditional dot ("`.`") notation when an object calls a procedure in a local sequential object. For example, a constraint server has a local object called `requestQueue`, and a constraint server invokes the procedure `empty` in this object by `requestQueue.empty`.

Check actions lock a constraint server in order to evaluate disabling constraints. The instance variable `currentId` is the CID of the check action that currently holds the lock to the server. If `currentId` is `NIL`, the constraint server is not locked. If a constraint server receives a query while it is not locked, the lock to the server is immediately granted to the check action of the query. The actual locking takes place in the `legal` procedure when `currentId` is assigned. A constraint server does not invoke its `legal` procedure until it is willing to be locked.

The queue `requestQueue` contains the queries waiting for the lock at a constraint server. If a constraint server receives a query with CID c_1 while it is locked by a check action C with CID c_2, there are three possible outcomes:

```
class ConstraintServer inherits Actor
  currentId,Messages,rootMessage,currentIndex := NIL,∅,NIL,0;
  requestQueue;

  method checkConstraints(m,id,inx)
    if currentId = NIL or currentId = id then reply legal(m,id,inx);
    else
      if id is older than currentId and all id's in requestQueue then
        requestQueue.put([m,id,inx,sender]);
      else reply kill;
  end checkConstraints;

  procedure legal(m,id,inx)
    currentId := id;
    if currentIndex ≠ inx then currentIndex,Messages := inx,∅;
    if inx = 0 then rootMessage := m;
    else Messages := Messages ∪ { m };
    if m satisfies all disable constraints
    then return yes;
    else return no;
  end legal;

  method abort(id,inx)
    if currentId = id then
      if (rootMessage ≠ NIL and inx = 0) or rootMessage = NIL
      then releaseLock();
  end abort;

  method commit(id)
    if currentId = id then
      execute triggers relative to Messages and rootMessage;
      releaseLock()
  end commit;

  procedure releaseLock()
    currentId,currentIndex,rootMessage := NIL,0,NIL;
    if not requestQueue.empty() then
      [m,id,inx,dest] := requestQueue.getOldest();
      reply legal(m,id,inx) to dest;
  end releaseLock;
end ConstraintServer;
```

Figure 5.13
Pseudocode for `ConstraintServer`

1. $c_1 = c_2$. The query with CID c_1 originates from a nested check action that has C as its top-level check action. In this case, the nested check action will inherit the lock from C and is allowed to proceed and test the constraints for the message.

2. c_1 is older than c_2 and the CID of all queries in requestQueue. Since older check actions may wait on younger check actions, the query is stored in a request queue for later processing.

3. c_1 is younger than either c_2 or the CID of one of the waiting queries in requestQueue. In this case, the check action with CID c_1 is preempted as part of the deadlock prevention scheme. The constraint server sends kill as a reply to the request.

Once a check action has locked a constraint server, it evaluates the disabling constraints for a message. The actual constraint evaluation takes place in the procedure called legal. The arguments to legal identify a message and the check action CA that is evaluating the disabling constraints for this message. The m argument is the message for which the disabling constraints must be evaluated. The id argument is the CID of CA, and the inx argument identifies CA as a specific check action with that CID. The inx variable is integer valued. If CA is a top-level check action, the value of inx is 0; otherwise the value of inx is a positive integer.

A nested check action may give rise to multiple requests sent to the same constraint server. For example, if a nested check action is trying to schedule an atomicity constraint with n patterns, there will be $n - 1$ participating objects that could potentially query the same constraint server to evaluate the disabling constraints for their leaf messages. The set Messages contains all the leaf messages that have been tested at a constraint server as part of the current nested check action. If the current check action is a top-level check action, the message being checked is a root message, and the set Messages is empty. Root messages are stored in the variable rootMessage.

A constraint server keeps track of the index of the current nested check action. This index is stored in the variable currentIndex. If a constraint server receives a request with an index that is different from the value stored in currentIndex, the set Messages becomes the empty set, and currentIndex becomes the new index.

A constraint server may receive abort messages from nested as well

as top-level check actions. If a top-level check action holds the lock
to the constraint server, an `abort` message from a nested check action
should not unlock the constraint server. In order to prevent a nested
check action from unlocking a constraint server that is locked by a top-
level check action, the `abort` method examines the value of the variable
`rootMessage`. If this variable is `NIL` there is no top-level check action,
and an abort message should release the lock. If there is a top-level
check action, only an `abort` message from the top-level check action
(with index 0) should release the lock.

The lock release at a constraint server takes place in the procedure
called `releaseLock`. The lock is released by assigning the variable
`currentId` to `NIL`. The `releaseLock` method also initiates processing
of the requests stored in the `requestQueue`; the request with the oldest
CID is chosen as the next request to be serviced.

Remember that in addition to disabling constraints, a constraint server
also contains the triggers of a synchronizer. The triggers must be executed when messages are dispatched. An object queries a constraint
server with respect to a given message if the server has either a trigger or
a disabling constraint, or both, that apply to the message. The variable
`rootMessage` and the set `Messages` together contain the messages for
which triggers must be executed if the check action with CID `currentId`
commits. The actual triggering takes place in the `commit` method. After
the triggers are executed, the `commit` method releases the lock to the
constraint server by calling the procedure `releaseLock`.

A check action may give rise to multiple `abort` or `commit` messages
sent to the same constraint server. For example, when a nested check
action commits, each participating object sends a `commit` message to all
the constraint servers that it has queried. A constraint server reacts to
the first `commit` message that it receives. Thus, the constraint server
may already be processing another request when it receives the rest of
the `commit` messages associated with the previous request. In order to
avoid the situation that an "old" `commit` message commits the current
check action, we test whether `currentId` is equal to `id` in the `commit`
method. The same consideration applies to the `abort` method.

5.5.3 Evaluating Atomicity Constraints

Having discussed the evaluation of disabling constraints, we now proceed
to examine the evaluation of atomicity constraints. An initiating object

---

procedure checkAtomic(m,id)
  inconclusive := **false**;
  if atomicList.empty() **then**
    return yes;
  for i := 1 **to** atomicList.size() **do**
    tup := atomicList.getAtomicRelation(i);
    send findMatch(tup,id,i) **to** destinations(tup) - { **self** };
    wait for replies;
    if *all replies are* yes **then**
      send commit(id) **to** destinations(tup);
      return yes;
    if *one of the replies is* no **then**
      send abort(id,i) **to** destinations(tup);
    else
      send abort(id,i) **to** destinations(tup);
      inconclusive := **true**;
  end for
  if inconclusive **then return** kill
  else return no,;
end checkAtomic;

Figure 5.14
Pseudocode for `checkAtomic`

evaluates the atomicity constraints for a root message by calling the
`checkAtomic` procedure. The pseudocode for this procedure is given in
figure 5.14. The procedure is called with two arguments: `m` and `id`. The
`m` argument is the message for which the atomicity constraints should be
checked; the `id` argument is the CID of the (nested) check action that
performs this constraint check.

If the atomic list for `m` is empty, the atomicity constraints are trivially
satisfied for `m`. Otherwise the atomic list is traversed in order to test
the atomicity constraints one at a time (the variable `i` iterates over the
indices of the list).

Given an index into the atomic list, the procedure `getAtomicRelation`
returns the tuple of patterns contained in the list element with this index. For a tuple of patterns, the procedure `destinations` returns a
set that contains the destination object of each pattern in the tuple (a
pattern "*o.m* **if** *e*" has *o* as destination object). This set of destination
objects enables the initiating object to determine the set of participating
objects.

The initiating object sends a findMatch message to each participating object. In response to this message, a participating object determines whether it has a legal leaf message for the atomicity constraint being evaluated. If all the participating objects respond yes, the constraint is satisfied, and the checkAtomic method returns yes and commits the check action. If one of the participating objects responds no, an abort message is sent to the participating objects, and the initiating object evaluates the next atomicity constraint in its atomic list. If the atomic list is exhausted without any constraint being satisfied, the initiating object concludes that the applicable atomicity constraints are not satisfied for the argument message, and no is returned.

If the initiating object receives a mix of yes and kill responses the evaluation is inconclusive: the evaluated atomicity constraint may or may not be satisfied, but this cannot be determined because one or more of the requests are preempted by the deadlock-prevention scheme. If an evaluation is inconclusive, the variable inconclusive is set to true. If the list is exhausted and one or more check attempts were inconclusive, kill is returned by checkAtomic.

The construction of CIDs requires that we distinguish between kill and no as results returned by checkAtomic. When no is returned, the local counter used to construct CIDs is incremented since the check action ran to completion. If, on the other hand, kill is returned, the check action was preempted, and the counter should not be incremented. The construction of CIDs is discussed further in section 5.5.4.

The initiating object plays the role of client, and the participating objects play the role of server. These client-server roles are relative to a specific check action. A client object in one check action may be a server object in another check action. The checkAtomic procedure describes the client aspect of objects. In the following, I give pseudocode for the methods and procedures that describe the server aspect of objects.

The pseudocode for the server aspect of objects is illustrated in figure 5.15. The interface of a participating object consists of three methods: findMatch, abort, and commit. When an initiating object evaluates an atomicity constraint, it sends a findMatch message to all the participating objects for that constraint. The findmatch method takes three arguments. The tup argument is a tuple of patterns; the id and inx arguments identify the nested check action that is trying to schedule

class ConstrainedObject **inherits** Actor
currentMessage,currentId := NIL,NIL;
requestQueue;

method findMatch(tup,id,inx)
pat := *the pattern in* tup *related to this object*;
if currentId = NIL **then reply** satisfied(pat,id,inx);
else
   if id *is older than* currentId *and all id's in* request queue **then**
   requestQueue.put([pat,id,inx,**sender**]);
   else reply kill;
end findMatch;

procedure satisfied(pat,id,inx)
if *there exists a message* m *in the input queue such that*
   matches(m,pat) *and* locallyEnabled(m)
then
   currentMessage,currentId := inputQueue.remove(m),id;
   return checkDisable(m,id,inx);
else return no;
end satisfied;

method commit(id)
   send commit(id) **to** servers(currentMessage);
   dispatch(currentMessage);
end commit;

method abort(id,inx)
   send abort(id,inx) **to** servers(currentMessage);
   inputQueue.enqueueChecked(currentMessage);
   releaseLock();
end abort;

procedure releaseLock()
   currentMessage,currentId := NIL,NIL;
   if not requestQueue.empty() **then**
   [tup,id,inx,dest] := requestQueue.getOldest();
   reply satisfied(tup,id,inx) **to** dest;
end releaseLock;
...
end ConstrainedObject;

Figure 5.15
Pseudocode for `ConstrainedObject`

the atomicity constraint. The interpretation of the `id` and `inx` arguments is similar to the `id` and `inx` arguments in the `checkConstraints`
method in constraint servers.

The `tup` argument of `findMatch` contains all the patterns that must
be matched in order to satisfy the atomicity constraint being tested.
If `findMatch` is invoked on a participating object *PO*, it extracts the
pattern in this tuple that has *PO* as destination. The extracted pattern
is bound to the name `pat`.

The `findMatch` method maintains a request queue in a manner similar to the `checkConstraints` method in constraint servers. The variable
`currentId` in a participating object is bound to the CID of the check action that currently locks the object. When a request invokes `findMatch`,
there are two possibilities:

- `currentId` = `NIL`. This means that the object is not locked, and the
  request is serviced immediately by calling the procedure `satisfied`.

- `currentId` $\neq$ `NIL`. This means that the object is locked. The request
  may or may not be allowed to wait in the request queue. For a request
  to be allowed to wait, the CID of this request must be older than the
  CID of all the requests stored in `requestQueue`.

The actual request processing at participating objects takes place
as part of the `satisfied` procedure. A participating object uses this
procedure to determine whether it can satisfy its part of the atomicity constraint being evaluated. It does so by checking whether there
is a message in its input queue that matches the pattern `pat`. In
searching for a matching message, `satisfied` evaluates the synchronization constraints for candidate messages by calling the procedure
`locallyEnabled`. If a matching message exists that satisfies the synchronization constraints, the participating object locks itself by assigning `currentId` to `id`. Moreover, the matching leaf message is bound to
the variable called `currentMessage`. The participating object then calls
`checkDisable` in order to evaluate the disabling constraints for this leaf
message. I gave the pseudocode for `checkDisable` in section 5.5.1.

A participating object is unlocked when it receives either an `abort`
or a `commit` message from the initiating object. The actual lock release
takes place in the procedure called `releaseLock`. As in the constraint

server class, the `releaseLock` procedure also initiates the processing of the next request in the request queue. Due to the deadlock prevention scheme, requests are extracted from the request queue so that the oldest request is extracted first.

If a participating object receives a `commit` message, it must dispatch the leaf message that is bound to the variable called `currentMessage`. This is accomplished by calling the `dispatch` procedure. Furthermore, the participating object must notify each constraint server that has a trigger for the leaf message. The participating object does this by sending a `commit` message to each element in the list returned by the `servers` procedure.

If a participating object receives an `abort` message, it must notify the queried constraint servers that the check action has aborted. Furthermore, `currentMessage` is put back into the input queue by the procedure called `enqueueChecked`.

In general, we distinguish between two kinds of messages in the input queue:

- *Checked*. Messages that are known not to satisfy the constraints in the current object and synchronizer state.

- *Waiting*. Messages that may satisfy the constraints in the current object and synchronizer state.

In this description, *constraints* refers to both synchronization constraints and constraints defined in synchronizers. A checked message can have failed to satisfy either kind of constraint. When first received, messages are marked as waiting. The procedure `enqueueChecked` adds a message to the input queue and marks the message as checked. Similarly, the procedure `enqueueWaiting` adds a message to the input queue and marks it as waiting.

When an object changes state (i.e., dispatches a message), it marks all messages in its input queue as waiting. State changes at constraint servers also cause messages to be marked as waiting. When a constraint server changes state (i.e., a trigger is activated), it notifies all the objects that it constrains. A notification indicates to these objects that the disabling constraints at a server may have changed status. In response to a notification from a constraint server, an object marks all messages in its input queue as waiting.

After a state change, either local or at a constraint server, an object marks all its messages as waiting even though only a subset of these messages may actually be affected by the state change. For example, the synchronization constraints for a specific message may depend only on a particular instance variable; however, this message is marked as waiting even if other instance variables are updated. In a library implementation of synchronization constraints, it is hard to avoid the potential inefficiency caused by marking all messages as waiting: a library implementation cannot determine which updates affect specific messages because it does not know the structure of applications. Constructing a scheme where only a subset of messages are marked as waiting requires support from a compiler that can statically analyze the application structure.

5.5.4 Evaluating Disabling and Atomicity Constraints

Given the above definitions of `checkDisable` and `checkAtomic`, I can now give the definition of a procedure called `checkMessage` that evaluates both disabling constraints and atomicity constraints for a given message. The pseudocode for `checkMessage` is given in figure 5.16.

To simplify the pseudocode, I do not describe the following aspects of constrained objects:

- *Message delivery.* I do not describe how the communication subsystem delivers messages to the input queue of an object. I describe only how an object evaluates the disabling and atomicity constraints for these messages.

- *Construction of CIDs.* I do not describe how object addresses and local counters are used to construct CIDs; I assume that CIDs are passed as argument to `checkMessage`.

- *Locking of initiating objects.* Initiating objects are locked when they evaluate the constraints for a message. I assume that an initiating object has already been locked when `checkMessage` is called.

The procedure `checkMessage` first evaluates the synchronization constraints for argument messages. If the synchronization constraints are satisfied, the procedure evaluates the disabling constraints. Finally, if the disabling constraints are also satisfied, the atomicity constraints are evaluated.

```
class ConstrainedObject inherits Actor
 inputQueue;

 procedure checkMessage(m,id)
   if not locallyEnabled(m) then inputQueue.enqueueChecked(m);
   else
     case checkDisable(m,id,0) of
     no : rejected(m);
     kill : killed(m);
     yes :
       case checkAtomic(m,id) of
       yes :
         send commit(id) to servers(m);
         dispatched(m);
       no :
         send abort(id,0) to servers(m);
         rejected(m);
       kill :
         send abort(id,0) to servers(m);
         killed(m);
       end case
     end case
   end checkMessage;

 procedure dispatched(m)
   incrementCounter();
   dispatch(m);
 end dispatched;

 procedure rejected(m)
   incrementCounter();
   inputQueue.enqueueChecked(m);
 end rejected;

 procedure killed(m)
   inputQueue.enqueueWaiting(m);
 end killed;
   ...
 end constrainedObject;
```

Figure 5.16
Pseudocode for `checkMessage`

The **dispatched** procedure dispatches messages. The **rejected** procedure is called when a message has been checked and does not satisfy the constraints. In this case, the message is put back into the input queue and marked as checked. Finally, the **killed** procedure is called whenever a check action is preempted.

The **incrementCounter** procedure increments the local counter used in construction of CIDs. This counter is incremented only if a check action runs to completion; that is, it is not preempted by the deadlock-prevention scheme. If a check action is preempted, the same CID is used for the next check action. By recycling CIDs, a preempted check action will eventually have an old enough CID, and it will not be preempted. As discussed further in section 5.7, recycling CIDs is one of the keys to ensure fairness.

5.5.5 Discussion

The above pseudocode illustrates the basic principles of the implementation, but it is a simplified and somewhat inefficient projection of the actual implementation. In this section, I describe some of the aspects that I have ignored, or overly simplified, in the pseudocode description.

The patterns of an atomicity constraint may depend on the state of the enclosing synchronizer. Because constraint servers contain the state of synchronizers, objects may need to communicate with constraint servers when they attempt to schedule a state-dependent atomicity constraint. For simplicity, the pseudocode ignores this communication between objects and constraint servers. In the following, I describe how this communication is handled in the implementation.

Assume that a pattern p in an atomicity constraint depends on the state of its enclosing synchronizer. Assume further that the constraint server cs represents this enclosing synchronizer. If o is the destination object of p and m is the destination method of p, we add cs to the server list of m in o. By adding cs to the server list, it appears to o as if m is subject to a disabling constraint, and o will query cs before it evaluates the state-dependent atomicity constraint. When o queries cs, it automatically obtains the state of cs, because we piggy-back the state of constraint servers onto the reply returned by **checkConstraints**. Moreover, when o queries cs, it locks cs while it evaluates the state-dependent atomicity constraint. This means that the state does not change while o evaluates the atomicity constraint.

The pseudocode describes constraint evaluation as if an object initiates only one check action at a time. In the actual implementation, an initiating object makes a distinction between "lightweight" check actions that involve only synchronization constraints and "heavyweight" check actions that involve disabling and atomicity constraints. An initiating object executes lightweight check actions independently and concurrently with heavyweight check actions. Concurrent execution of lightweight and heavyweight check actions reduces the impact of synchronizers on messages that are not constrained by synchronizers.

The concurrency between lightweight and heavyweight check actions implies that the state of an object may change while a heavyweight check action is executing. Hence, objects must recheck their synchronization constraints at the end of a heavyweight check action to ensure that the synchronization constraints are still satisfied for root and leaf messages.

Objects have both a client and a server aspect. Initiating objects are clients, and participating objects are servers. The pseudocode describes the client and server aspects of an object as if they were independent. In the actual implementation, an object cannot be both client and server at the same time. If an object initiates a check action, that check action locks the object, and the object cannot play the role of participating object for the duration of this check action. Similarly, if an object participates in a check action initiated by another object, this check action will lock the object, and the object cannot initiate check actions itself.

In the pseudocode, objects that send multiple concurrent requests always wait for *all* the replies to arrive before they continue their computation. In many cases, this reply synchronization is overly restrictive and inefficient. In the actual implementation, objects often continue after receiving only a subset of the replies. For example, the method `checkDisable` sends a request to multiple constraint servers in order to test the applicable disabling constraints. After receiving one negative reply, the method can safely continue and abort the check action.

Not waiting for all replies implies that the replies from two different check actions may overlap at objects. For example, when an object continues after receiving one negative reply, it may receive the rest of the replies after it initiates another check action. In the implementation we tag each reply with the CID of its associated check action, making it possible to distinguish between replies sent as part of different check actions.

In the pseudocode, a top-level check action always locks a constraint server when it tests the disabling constraints for a message. In the actual implementation, a top-level check action locks a server only if the constraints are actually satisfied; if a message does not satisfy the disabling constraints, the server is not locked.

In the pseudocode, state changes at both objects and constraint servers cause messages to be marked as waiting so that they can be rechecked. In the actual implementation, we do not apply such marking to messages that are subject only to state-independent atomicity constraints. State changes will not affect the legality of such messages.

In the implementation, we distinguish between simple patterns of the form "*o.m*" and complex patterns "*o.m* if *e*." A number of messages that are constrained by a simple pattern will either all be legal or all be illegal. If a message is checked to be illegal according to a simple pattern, we mark all messages for the same method as checked. By marking all messages as checked, we effectively check multiple messages by means of the same check action.

5.6   Serializability

A check action must be an atomic, indivisible occurrence. As in most database systems, I use *serializability* as the semantics of atomicity. In the following I argue that check actions are serializable; they appear to have happened serially, one at a time, in some unspecified order. I show that the locking scheme used by check actions satisfies the rules for two-phase locking for nested transactions as defined by Moss [Mos85].

Let us reconsider the way in which check actions are nested. It is a top-level check action when an initiating object evaluates the disabling constraints for a root message. It is a nested check action when an initiating object evaluates the atomicity constraints for a root message. It is part of an existing nested check action when a participating object evaluates the disabling constraints for a leaf message.

A nested check action inherits the locks held by its top-level check action. Furthermore, a nested check action can abort independently: its top-level check action does not have to abort also. In particular, when a nested check action aborts, it does not release the locks that are also held by its top-level check action.

Moss [Mos85] gives rules that provide two-phase locking for nested transactions. I reformulate the rules as they apply to our specific case with at most one level of nesting:

1. An action may acquire a lock if no other action holds that lock.

2. An action must hold the lock to an entity before manipulating the entity.

3. An action may not acquire locks if it has released any locks.

4. An action may release locks at any time.

5. An action may acquire an already held lock only if the only other holder is its top-level action.

6. When a nested action commits, its top-level action inherits all its locks.

7. When a nested action aborts, all its locks are released. If a top-level action holds any of the locks, it continues to do so.

The first four rules are the usual two-phase locking rules for nonnested transactions. These rules are clearly satisfied by the implementation. I will comment only on the satisfaction of the last three rules, which are specific to nesting.

Rule 5 states that lock sharing may take place only between a top-level check action and *one* of its nested check actions; two nested check actions may not simultaneously share a lock with their top-level check action. Since the atomicity constraints for a message are checked one at a time, a top-level check action initiates at most one nested check action at a time; nested check actions are never concurrent in the implementation. This one-to-one correspondence between nested and top-level check actions ensures that two nested check actions will never inherit the same lock. Therefore, the implementation satisfies rule 5.

Rule 6 is concerned with the propagation of locks from a nested check action to its top-level check action. When a nested check action commits, its top-level check action must take over its locks. The purpose of rule 6 is to ensure that the effect of a nested check action is not visible to the outside world until its top-level check action is done. In our system, a nested check action commits only if its top-level check action commits. In other words, a nested check action does not independently commit. Thus, the lock propagation required by rule 6 is satisfied by our implementation.

Rule 7 is concerned with the release of locks by a nested check action. If a nested check action shares a lock with its top-level check action, the top-level check action should continue to hold this lock even if the nested check action aborts and releases its locks. In our implementation, lock sharing takes place at constraint servers: if an initiating object locks a constraint server and a participating object queries the same constraint server, the objects will share the lock to the server. Satisfaction of rule 7 is ensured by the way in which constraint servers implement **abort**. The lock to a server is not released by **abort** if the **abort** message originates from a nested check action *and* there is a top-level check action that holds the lock to the server. The variable **rootMessage** in a constraint server indicates whether a top-level check action holds the lock to the server.

5.7 Fairness

In this section I analyze the fairness of the implementation. In the implementation, fairness is a property related to the eventual dispatch of messages. Inspired by Francez [Fra86], I distinguish between weak and strong fairness:

- *Weak fairness.* An object will eventually dispatch a message that *remains* (continuously) legal after some instant in time.

- *Strong fairness.* An object will eventually dispatch a message that is legal *infinitely often* after some instant in time.

Weak and strong fairness capture two kinds of circumstances under which the implementation guarantees eventual message dispatch. With weak fairness, the implementation guarantees eventual dispatch of a message only if there is an instant in time after which the message is permanently legal. With strong fairness, the implementation guarantees eventual dispatch of a message under the more general condition that there is an instant in time after which the message is legal during certain time intervals, and these intervals keep reoccuring ad infinitum. Weak and strong fairness capture two degrees of fairness. Strong fairness implies weak fairness since it guarantees eventual dispatch under a more general condition.

In the following I illustrate the concepts of weak and strong fairness by example synchronizers. Section 5.7.1 illustrates weak fairness, and section 5.7.2 illustrates strong fairness. Section 5.7.3 describes the notion of fairness that our implementation provides.

5.7.1 Weak Fairness

Consider the cause synchronizer in figure 5.17 that enforces a disabling constraint on m messages destined for the object p. p cannot dispatch these messages until the object o has dispatched an m message. If the cause synchronizer is the only constraint that applies to p, and if p has an m message in its input queue, the dispatch of an m message by o will constitute "an instant in time," after which p's m message remains legal. The implementation is weakly fair if it guarantees that p will eventually dispatch its m message.

5.7.2 Strong Fairness

Consider the choice synchronizer in figure 5.18. This synchronizer applies to the objects o, p, and q. Each of these objects has a method called m. When o dispatches an m message, either p or q may also dispatch an m message. Assume that the choice synchronizer is the only constraint on o, p, and q, that p has an m message in its input queue, and that an infinite stream of m messages is sent to o and q. The m message at p is then legal each time o dispatches an m message. But

```
synchronizer cause(o,p)
    i := 0;

  trigger
    o.m → { i := 1; };
  disable
    p.m if i = 0;
end cause;
```

Figure 5.17
A synchronizer that illustrates weak fairness

```
synchronizer choice(o,p,q)
   i := 0;

   trigger
     o.m → { i := 1; };
     p.m → { i := 0; };
     q.m → { i := 0; };
   disable
     p.m if i = 0;
     q.m if i = 0;
end choice;
```

Figure 5.18
A synchronizer that illustrates strong fairness

each time q dispatches an m message, the m message at p will no longer
be legal. Hence, as o and q dispatch m messages, the m message at p will
alternate between legal and illegal, and this alternation will continue ad
infinitum. The implementation is strongly fair if it guarantees that p
will eventually dispatch its m message under these circumstances.

5.7.3 Our Notion of Fairness

Our implementation is weakly fair but not strongly fair. In the following I briefly outline the main issues involved in constructing a weakly
fair implementation. I also point out the difficulties associated with
guaranteeing strong fairness in our implementation framework.

I identify only the main issues in implementing a weakly fair algorithm; giving a complete proof of weak fairness would involve extensive
case analysis and would not provide significant new insights about our
implementation principles. In our implementation, weak fairness is a
result of two properties: legal messages will eventually be checked, and
a check action will eventually complete without being preempted.

Eventual checking of legal messages is ensured by the following two
properties of our implementation:

1. *A legal message will eventually be marked as waiting.* Consider a legal
   message at an object o. When first received, messages are marked as

waiting. Hence, if the message was legal when *o* received it, this property is trivially satisfied. If the message was illegal when *o* received it, there must have been a state change that caused the message to become legal. This state change could have occurred at either a synchronizer or at *o*. If the state change occurred at *o*, the message would have been marked as waiting. This is because, in general, any state change is caused by the dispatch of a message, and any message dispatch causes all messages in the input queue to be marked as waiting. If, instead, the state change occurred at a synchronizer, the synchronizer would have notified *o* about the state change, and *o* would have marked all messages as waiting in response to this notification.

2. *Waiting messages will eventually result in a check action.* Newly arrived messages are appended to the input queue, and the search for waiting messages is initiated at the front of the queue. Furthermore, our implementation ensures that an object does not spend all its time finding leaf messages for check actions initiated by other objects. After consecutively searching for a certain number of leaf messages, an object examines its input queue to see if any messages are marked as waiting.

A check action will eventually complete without being preempted. Assume that an object *o* initiates a check action that is preempted. In this case, the check action's root message is put back into *o*'s input queue and marked as waiting. Since the message is marked as waiting, it will be rechecked later. Furthermore, *o* will reuse the same CID for future check actions until a check action runs to completion. Other objects whose check actions run to completion will use younger and younger CIDs for their check actions. Eventually the CID associated with *o* will be old enough (relatively speaking) to not get preempted.

Having explained the main principles of our weakly fair implementation, I justify in the following why the implementation does not provide strong fairness. First, let us examine how the implementation behaves with respect to the choice synchronizer in figure 5.18. In the implementation, this synchronizer is represented by a constraint server, say, cs. When o dispatches an m message, the triggers of cs are executed, and p and q are notified of this state change at cs. This notification causes p and q to mark all messages in their input queues as waiting. If p and q both have an m message, both will try to test the disabling constraints by querying cs. The choice between p and q is then determined by who first obtains the lock to cs. In this case, the notification scheme creates a "race" between p and q. In the implementation, this race may favor p indefinitely; for example, p may be favored if cs and p are collocated on the same node, since the communication between p and cs will presumably be faster than the communication between q and cs.

It would seem that the race condition created by the notification scheme could be eliminated by notifying the constrained objects one at a time in a round robin fashion. However, such a notification scheme would not be sufficient to ensure strong fairness in the general case. For example, assume that p and q are subject to two synchronizers represented by the constraint servers cs1 and cs2 in figure 5.19. If the same message dispatch causes a state change at both cs1 and cs2, the round robin approach would not guarantee strong fairness: cs1 could notify p, and cs2 could notify q. In this situation we would still get a race condition between p and q.

The conclusion is that strong fairness requires cooperation between constraint servers in their notification scheme. As suggested by the simple example above, implementing strong fairness will lead to some notion of centralized "scheduling" of check actions. In other words, im-

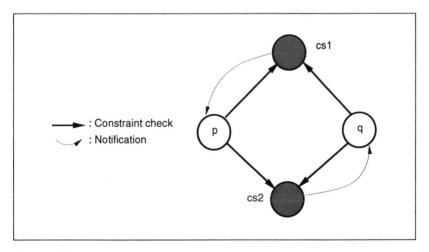

Figure 5.19
Round robin notification with overlapping constraint servers

plementing strong fairness potentially results in significant loss of concurrency. Whether it is desirable to pay the price for strong fairness is an application-specific issue. I have chosen not to incorporate strong fairness in the general-purpose implementation.

Part of the difficulty associated with implementing strong fairness is due to the fact that our implementation is generic; it does not make any assumptions about the specific constraints being evaluated. In specific cases, such as that of the `choice` synchronizer described above, strong fairness could be implemented using relatively simple techniques. In order to take advantage of such techniques, it is necessary to employ static analysis techniques and have a compiler give hints to the run-time system about the nature of enforced constraints.

5.8   Message Complexity

Message complexity is the number of messages sent as part of a check action. We determine the worst-case message complexity for check actions based on the following quantities:

S =   synchronizers per object
P =   patterns per atomicity constraint
A =   atomicity constraints per message

Checking the disabling constraints for a given message m involves a two-phase commit protocol with all the constraint servers in m's server list. In the worst case, m's server list contains S constraint servers. Since a two-phase commit protocol requires 3 messages, the message complexity of checking the disabling constraints for m is $3S$ in the worst case.

When evaluating the atomicity constraints for a message, there are $P - 1$ participating objects in the worst case. The initiating object carries out a two-phase commit protocol with each participating object, requiring a total of $3(P-1)$ messages. At each of the $P-1$ participating objects, a leaf message may be constrained by disabling constraints. In the worst case, each of the $P-1$ participating objects will initiate a two-phase commit with S constraint servers. The total message complexity per atomicity constraint is then $3S(P-1) + 3(P-1)$. In the worst-case scenario, it is necessary to evaluate A atomicity constraints, each with this complexity.

All in all, evaluating the disabling and atomicity constraints for a given message has the following worst-case message complexity:

$$
\begin{aligned}
\text{Messages per check action} \quad &= \quad 3S + A(3(P-1) + 3S(P-1)) \\
&= \quad 3S + A(3 + 3S)(P-1)
\end{aligned}
$$

Notice that the above estimate includes only messages sent as part of check actions. Notification messages are not included. Notification initiated by a given constraint server requires one message per constrained object.

5.9   Performance

I use the dispatch rate of check actions as a performance metric. The dispatch rate is the percentage of check actions that are committed. This rate is an indication of the efficiency of the algorithms used. An ideal algorithm initiates only check actions that result in message dispatch. However, an ideal algorithm is unrealistic: in the general case, an ideal algorithm requires global control by one centralized scheduler. In practice, the challenge is to design an algorithm that combines autonomy between objects with a reasonable dispatch rate.

In order to determine the dispatch rate and analyze the impact of different heuristics on the dispatch rate, we measure the outcome of check actions. A check action can have three possible outcomes:

- *Dispatch*. The check action resulted in message dispatch. This means that the check action committed.

- *Rejection*. The check action determined that the root message did not satisfy the constraints. This means that the check action aborted.

- *Preemption*. The check action collided with another check action at a shared resource. The check action was aborted by the deadlock-prevention algorithm.

The dispatch rate is the rate between dispatched check action on the one hand, and rejected and preempted check actions on the other. We have measured the dispatch rate of the implementation for different workloads generated by two different applications. Each application captures a prototypical coordination scheme. We performed the measurements on a cluster of three DEC workstations interconnected by Ethernet. In the experiments, objects are distributed as evenly as possible across the network.

Resources are requested by a number of consumers. After being granted a resource, a consumer holds that resource for a period of time and then releases it.

Application 1 Cooperating Resource Administrators
As described in example 4, a resource administrator controls the allocation of shared resources. A resource administrator has a synchronization constraint that blocks allocation requests if no resources are available.

In the cooperating administrators application, a number of resource consumers request resources from a group of resource administrators. After being granted a resource, a consumer holds that resource for a period of time and then releases it. The group of administrators coordinate their allocation so that there is a bound on the number of resources allocated *collectively* by the group. This coordination is described by the synchronizer in figure 5.20. The name `administrators` is a set that contains the addresses of the administrators in the group. The name `MAX` denotes the maximum number of resources that may be allocated collectively by the group. The state of the synchronizer consists of the

```
synchronizer collectiveAllocation(administrators,bound)
    allocated := 0;

  for adm in administrators
    trigger
        adm.release → { allocated := allocated - 1 };
        adm.request → { allocated := allocated + 1 };
  for adm in administrators
    disable
        adm.request if allocated ≥ MAX;
end collectiveAllocation;
```

Figure 5.20
Synchronizer that enforces bound on collective allocation of resources

variable `allocated`. This variable is updated by the synchronizer so that its value reflects the number of resources currently allocated. The disabling constraint in the synchronizer prevents allocation if the value of `allocated` is greater than or equal to `MAX`. The trigger in the synchronizer increments the value of `allocated` each time a resource is released. The cooperating resource administrators application is prototypical in that it captures temporally ordered message dispatch for a group of objects.

At the implementation level, check actions occur whenever an administrator wants to dispatch a `request` message. In order to dispatch such messages, the administrator initiates a check action that queries the constraint server representing the `administrators` synchronizer.

I generated different workloads by varying the following parameters:

A—administrators
C—consumers per administrator
R—resources per administrator
B—collective bound enforced by the synchronizer

Each administrator has the same number of resources and the same number of consumers. In all workloads, each consumer allocates only one resource, and all consumers hold a resource for the same amount of time. For different values of these parameters, I measured the number of check actions in each of the three categories—dispatched, rejected, and preempted—and computed the dispatch rate.

The breakdown of check actions is shown in table 5.1. Because of the nondeterminism involved, the data represent average values from repeated measurements.

First, notice that for each workload, the absolute number of dispatched check actions is equal to $2 * C * A$: each request and release message processed by an administrator yields a dispatched check action. The first three workloads illustrate the dispatch rate when the collective bound is increased. As expected, increasing the bound reduces the number of rejections. At the same time, an increased bound increases the concurrency among the consumers and therefore gives rise to more check actions. This increase in check actions results in more collisions and therefore more preempted check actions. The last three workloads represent different ways to reduce the number of concurrent check actions.

workload	1	2	3	4	5	6
A	5	5	5	3	5	5
C	6	6	6	6	4	6
R	4	4	4	4	4	2
B	3	7	10	7	7	7
dispatched	60	60	60	36	40	60
rejected	62	46	26	5	18	21
preempted	169	195	228	76	112	140
% dispatched	21 %	20 %	19 %	31 %	24 %	27 %

Table 5.1
Check actions initiated by administrators

In workload 4, the number of administrators is decreased, and in workload 5, the number of consumers is decreased. In both cases, the collision rate drops. Finally, the last workload reduces the set of resources available at administrators. A reduced set of resources results in a reduced number of concurrent consumers and thereby a reduced collision rate.

As shown by the data, the number of collisions is relatively high for this application. The high collision rate is partly due to the strategy used when check actions are preempted. As described in the pseudocode for killed in figure 5.16, the root message of a preempted check action is put back into the input queue and marked as waiting. Because the message is marked as waiting, it will be rechecked at a later time. However, there is no guarantee that the message is not rechecked right away. If the message is the only one in the input queue, it will indeed be rechecked immediately in our implementation. Consequently, a preempted check action can lead to busy waiting where checking the same message is preempted over and over again. Although the preempted message will eventually be checked, the resulting busy waiting is inefficient.

In order to quantify the inefficiency caused by busy waiting, I have implemented a scheme under which preempted messages do not busy wait. In this alternative implementation, objects can be suspended and resumed. An object is suspended when it has a check action preempted at a constraint server, and it is resumed when the constraint server is ready to process the next request. If an object is suspended, it cannot initiate check actions until it is resumed.

workload	1	2	3	4	5	6
A	5	5	5	3	5	5
C	6	6	6	6	4	6
R	4	4	4	4	4	2
B	3	7	10	7	7	7
dispatched	60	60	60	36	40	60
rejected	48	23	15	3	10	9
preempted	52	88	112	28	63	78
% dispatched	38 %	35 %	32 %	54 %	35 %	41 %
% improvement	17 %	15 %	13 %	30 %	11 %	14 %

Table 5.2
Check actions initiated by administrators with suspension of objects

I ran an implementation that uses suspension rather than busy-wait for the same workloads used in table 5.1. The resulting measurement data are shown in table 5.2.

As expected, the number of collisions is reduced when objects are suspended rather than busy-wait. I compare the dispatch rate with busy-waiting to the dispatch rate with suspension. The improvement in dispatch rate is given in table 5.2.

Multiple objects may have a check action preempted at the same constraint server. When these objects are resumed, they all reinitiate their check action, which may lead to collisions at the server. Rather than resume all the objects at the same time, we could instead resume one object at a time and avoid these collisions. I have constructed an implementation that uses single-object resumption. Again, the same workloads are used in measuring the performance of the implementation. The results obtained from single-object resumption are presented in figure 5.3. As above, I have calculated the improvement in dispatch rate relative to the results in table 5.1.

As shown by the data in table 5.3, collisions have a significant impact on the dispatch rate. Collisions also occur in connection with the notification of state changes. Each time a constraint server changes state, the constrained objects are notified so that they can recheck their messages. Rather than notify all the constrained objects at the same time, a constraint server could notify the constrained objects one at a time

workload	1	2	3	4	5	6
A	5	5	5	3	5	5
C	6	6	6	6	4	6
R	4	4	4	4	4	2
B	3	7	10	7	7	7
dispatched	60	60	60	36	40	60
rejected	38	20	13	4	8	8
preempted	25	39	47	11	25	39
% dispatched	49 %	50 %	50 %	71 %	55 %	56 %
% improvement	28 %	30 %	31 %	40 %	31 %	29 %

Table 5.3
Check actions initiated by administrators with single-object resumption

in a manner similar to the single-object resumption scheme. Since the situations are similar, I do not present empirical data for single-object notification.

Although collisions are avoided, single-object notification is a trade-off: with single-object notification, the available concurrency is reduced. In order for single-object notification to be an improvement, there must be a high probability that the notified objects actually have messages to check. Otherwise objects with messages to check can end up waiting for notification of other objects that do not have messages to check. □

Application 2 Dining Philosophers
This application is the dining philosophers as described in example 6. A number of philosophers share a number of chopsticks. The number of chopsticks and the number of philosophers is the same, and a philosopher needs two chopsticks in order to eat. The philosophers need to coordinate their access to the chopsticks in order to avoid deadlocks and starvation.

A chopstick has a `pick` method that is invoked by philosophers in order to access the chopstick. When a philosopher is done using a chopstick, he invokes the `drop` method on the chopstick. Access to the chopsticks can be coordinated by a synchronizer enforced on the `pick` method of chopsticks. A possible synchronizer is depicted in figure 5.21. The synchronizer enforces an atomicity constraint on two chopsticks. There is one

```
synchronizer pickUp(c1,c2,phil)
  atomic
    (c1.pick(p1) if p1 = phil, c2.pick(p2) if p2 = phil);
  end pickUp;
```

Figure 5.21
A synchronizer that provides atomic access of chopsticks

such synchronizer for each philosopher, guaranteeing that a philosopher always accesses either two chopsticks or no chopsticks. Each chopstick is subject to two synchronizers: one for the philosopher to the left of the chopstick, and one for the philosopher to the right of the chopstick.

In running the dining philosophers application, I varied the number of entities (philosophers and chopsticks) and the number of times that a philosopher accesses his chopsticks. The data obtained are shown in table 5.4. Again, the data represent average values of repeated test runs.

workload	1	2	3	4	5
entities	3	4	5	6	7
dispatched	9	16	25	36	49
rejected	4	7	14	23	28
preempted	30	64	124	223	151
% dispatched	21 %	18 %	15 %	13 %	21 %

Table 5.4
Check actions initiated by chopsticks

Notice that with X entities being accessed Y times, we will get $X * Y$ dispatched check actions. The main source of rejected and preempted check actions is the symmetry with which two chopstick objects attempt to schedule the same atomicity constraint. When a philosopher object wants to eat, it sends a `pick` message to two chopsticks. Upon receipt of these messages, the chopsticks will then attempt to schedule the same atomicity constraint. If both chopsticks simultaneously initiate a check action to schedule the same atomicity constraint, one of these check actions will be preempted.

In general, it would be desirable to avoid symmetric evaluation of atomicity constraints and thereby reduce the number of preempted check actions. One (naive) way to avoid the symmetry would be, for each atomicity constraint, to appoint one object as "initiator" for the constraint, so that only the initiator is allowed to evaluate the constraint. However, in order to determine when to evaluate a constraint, an initiator object would need to know the content of the input queues at the other objects subject to the constraint. Keeping such cross-object information up to date is complicated by the fact that the same message may be subject to multiple atomicity constraints.

Rather than avoid symmetric evaluation in general, I have implemented a scheme to avoid symmetric evaluation for atomicity constraints that do not depend on the state of their enclosing synchronizer. If a message is affected only by state-independent atomicity constraints, its legality will not be affected by state changes. In the nonsymmetric implementation, a message that is affected only by state-independent atomicity constraints and has unsuccessfully been checked against these constraints is enqueued in a special message queue. Messages in the special queue are not marked as waiting after state changes and are therefore not rechecked after state changes. Thus, since the messages in the special queue are not rechecked, they cannot be root messages for check actions; they can only be leaf messages for check actions. Having a special category of messages that can only be leaf messages avoids symmetric evaluation.

I ran the dining philosophers workloads with a nonsymmetric implementation. The atomicity constraint for `pick` messages is state-independent. However, `pick` messages are also affected by synchronization constraints at chopsticks. Although the implementation correctly handles this state dependence, the details are rather elaborate and not described here. The results of running the nonsymmetric implementation are shown in table 5.5.

With the nonsymmetric implementation, we avoid a number of collisions that would otherwise result in preemption. When a philosopher is done eating, he drops two chopsticks. These drop actions result in a state change at both chopsticks. With the symmetric implementation, these state changes would, with high probability, result in two simultaneous check actions evaluating the same atomicity constraint. With the nonsymmetric implementation, only one check action is initiated. □

workload	1	2	3	4	5
entities	3	4	5	6	7
dispatched	9	16	25	36	49
rejected	5	6	12	23	27
preempted	19	55	93	85	99
% dispatched	27 %	21 %	19 %	25 %	28 %
% improvement	6 %	3 %	4 %	12 %	7 %

Table 5.5
Check actions initiated by chopsticks without rechecking after state changes

As the measurements show, the strategy used to determine when to recheck messages is an important factor in the overall performance of the algorithm. The challenge is to avoid excessive rechecking without sequentializing the check actions initiated by multiple objects. For example, constraint servers need to notify the constrained objects about state changes. Either all objects can be notified concurrently or the objects can be notified one at a time in a round robin fashion. Concurrent notification may lead to collisions, but round robin notification leads to sequential execution.

Which strategy to use for rechecking depends to a large extent on the application domain. For example, in connection with notification of state changes, certain state changes affect only a specific subset of the constrained objects. In such cases, it is desirable to notify only the affected subset. The problem we are facing is that our implementation is part of a library and therefore general; it does not know anything about the concrete application being coordinated. Hence, it is not possible to apply application-specific optimizations such as notifying only a subset of objects.

As already noted in section 5.7, an interesting topic for future work is to design a compiler for synchronizers and use static analysis techniques to recognize special cases. With static analysis techniques, the implementation would not have to rely exclusively on general strategies. Instead, a customized implementation could be provided for special cases. For example, it would be possible to implement a more finely-grained notification scheme that notifies only the objects that are actually affected by state changes at a synchronizer.

5.10   Possible Extensions

In this section I discuss a number of ways in which our implementation
can be extended. Since my goal was to develop a prototype implementation of synchronizers and synchronization constraints, I have chosen
not to pursue these extensions.

5.10.1   Migration

The BROADWAY library provides a facility for specifying the placement
of objects. Along the same lines, I provide a way to specify the placement of constraint servers. When instantiating a synchronizer, the programmer can either specify a node in the network on which to place the
constraint server, or specify an object and the constraint server will be
placed on the same node as the object. Given this functionality it is up
to the programmer to determine manually the placement of constraint
servers.

Once allocated, a constraint server cannot be migrated to a different
location. However, in some cases the optimal placement of a constraint
server changes over time. For example, the computation may go through
phases, and the optimal placement of constraint servers may not be the
same across phases. One possible extension would be to implement
migration of constraint servers and provide the programmer with constructs to control the migration of constraint servers.

Recent work within the Actor framework allows the specification of
migration and placement strategies for concurrent objects as modular
entities [AKP94, Pan96]. The migration and placement strategies can
be specified separate from the logics of a concurrent algorithm.

Our implementation does not present any inherent complications with
respect to migration. In particular, there is nothing that prevents application of traditional or modular techniques for migration and placement.

5.10.2   Fault Tolerance

I did not design the implementation to be fault tolerant. If a constraint
server fails, the constrained objects will not be able to dispatch messages that are subject to disabling constraints and triggers. Failure of
a constrained object will have a more local effect than failure of a constraint server. It will not be possible to schedule atomicity constraints

that require participation of a failed object. However, other objects can still evaluate disabling constraints and execute triggers.

There is nothing that prevents us from utilizing general techniques, such as replication and primary backup, to increase the availability of constraint servers. In fact, the BROADWAY library abstractions provide a flexible meta-architecture that supports the development, and transparent installation, of modular fault tolerant protocols [SA94]. As for migration, the conclusion is that our implementation does not present any new complications with respect to fault tolerance. It is possible to employ existing and general-purpose fault tolerance techniques.

5.10.3 Garbage Collection

In order to utilize resources more efficiently, it is desirable to garbage-collect obsolete synchronizers, those whose operation is complete and whose constraints no longer delay messages. For example, the `robots` synchronizer in example 7, in chapter 3 applies to specific cross-robot movements; when a cross-robot movement is complete, the attached synchronizer has served its purpose. It would be desirable to garbage-collect synchronizers when they are done. Garbage collection would not affect the functionality of an application but might affect its performance.

Implementing garbage collection of synchronizers is an open research problem. It is difficult to determine when a synchronizer has served its purpose. Recent work addresses the issue of garbage collecting distributed objects within the Actor framework [KWN90, VAT92]. However, these techniques use reachability as the obsolescence criterion for objects. Reachability cannot be used to garbage collect synchronizers: the duration of a synchronizer is determined by the logic of the specified constraints in the synchronizer, not by whether the synchronizer is reachable.

5.11 Alternatives

Anyone developing an implementation is faced with a number of basic design decisions. In this section, I outline a number of alternatives that I considered but decided against implementing. I describe these alternatives in order to convey some of the insights that I have gained in developing the implementation.

5.11.1   Communication with Constraint Servers

I considered changing the functionality of constraint servers so that objects could obtain the state of a server instead of inquire about the legality of specific messages. Given the state of the involved constraint servers, an object could evaluate the applicable disabling constraints locally. Furthermore, an object could evaluate the disabling constraints for all messages in its input queue as part of the same check action. This would reduce the message traffic between objects and constraint servers. However, since multiple messages may be checked as part of the same check action, constraint servers would be locked for longer periods of time. Another drawback is that an object would need to obtain the state of all constraint servers that constrain the object. Otherwise the object would not be able to check all messages as part of the same action. In contrast, our implementation locks only a subset of the constraint servers, namely, the servers that constrain a specific message.

5.11.2   Deadlocks

Deadlocks could be detected by time-outs instead of prevented by wait-die. With time-outs, an object starts a timer when it sends a request to another object. After a certain period, the timer expires, and it notifies the object. If the object receives a reply before the timer expires, the object resets the timer. If an object is notified by a timer, the object assumes that the request has deadlocked and the object starts to take corrective actions to break the deadlock; that is, the object can send a message that kills the request.

Due to the dynamic and unpredictable nature of check actions, the expiration time of timers would have to be long. Having long expiration times implies that deadlocks can exist for long periods before being detected. Whether to prevent or detect deadlocks depends on the frequency of deadlock situations. If deadlocks occur often, it is better to prevent them; if deadlocks are rare, it is better to detect them and take corrective actions. With my notification scheme for state changes at constraint servers, it is not appropriate to assume that deadlocks are rare. The reason is that all the constrained objects are notified of any state change at a constraint server. Hence, multiple objects will typically compete for the same constraint servers simultaneously. The resulting race condition creates a potential for deadlocks.

5.11.3   Concurrent Check Actions

I considered allowing an object to initiate multiple check actions concurrently. However, if the check actions overlap at constraint servers, concurrent initiation leads to contention for the same locks between the check actions. Multiple check actions are efficient only if they access different constraint servers. Whether this is the case is highly application specific.

5.11.4   Optimistic Concurrency Control

Multiple check actions may concurrently access the same shared entity, such as a constraint server or a participating object. Unless precautions are taken, check actions may collide at a shared entity and bring that entity into an inconsistent state. I employ concurrency control in order to avoid such inconsistencies and ensure serializability of check actions.

In my implementation, concurrency control is achieved by two-phase locking. Two-phase locking is a pessimistic approach because collisions are prevented. With two-phase locking, check actions gain exclusive access to shared entities. In particular, check actions never overlap at a shared entity. Thus, two-phase locking prevents shared entities, such as constraint servers, from concurrently processing multiple check actions.

I considered using a more optimistic approach in which check actions could overlap at shared entities. With the optimistic approach, collisions would be detected rather than prevented. With the optimistic approach, check actions would never be blocked at shared entities. Instead, check actions would have to be certified as serializable before they would be allowed to commit. Although certification could be done locally at each shared entity, the certification process would increase the message complexity of check actions by two messages per shared entity: a `certify` message sent to each entity and a reply sent back to the requesting object.

The choice between two-phase locking and certification depends on the structure of check actions. The question is whether the increase in concurrency that certification provides is big enough to justify the increased message complexity. In the following I shall discuss this trade-off relative to the expected structure of check actions in our implementation.

Let us assume that check actions are serialized by certification instead of locking. Consider two check actions C_1 and C_2 that involve the same shared entity S. With certification at S, there are three possible scenarios:

1. C_1 and C_2 do not overlap.

2. C_1 and C_2 overlap but do not collide. In other words, both C_1 and C_2 are certified as legal according to the serializability constraint.

3. C_1 and C_2 overlap and collide. In this case, either C_1 or C_2 cannot be certified as serializable and must be aborted for that reason.

It is scenario 2 that would favor certification because it allows concurrent execution without collision. Scenarios 1 and 3 would be handled more efficiently with a pessimistic approach: the cost of scenario 1 under both schemes is equal to the cost of executing the communication protocol associated with check actions and, as I have mentioned, this communication protocol has a higher message complexity under the optimistic scheme. For scenario 3 under a pessimistic scheme, one of the check actions would be blocked waiting to obtain a lock on S. Under an optimistic scheme, scenario 3 would result in abortion. Since blocking is more efficient than aborting, conflicts are handled more efficiently under a pessimistic approach.

For the optimistic approach to be preferable, scenario 2 must be frequent enough to justify the increased cost of scenarios 1 and 3. Whether this is the case ultimately depends on the application domain. But we can, in general, expect that overlapping check actions will collide frequently. Overlapping check actions will collide if they modify state, and check actions will typically modify state, either through triggers or message dispatch. My conjecture is that scenario 2 is not a frequent occurrence except in some specialized applications. Thus, I have chosen a pessimistic rather than an optimistic approach to concurrency control.

My findings are similar to the conventional wisdom in database systems. Optimistic concurrency control is typically employed in situations that involve large object pools and irregular transactions manipulating those objects. In such systems, collision can be assumed to be infrequent. My situation is a contrast: a small number of entities are heavily shared by transactions with a simple, regular structure.

5.11.5   Distributed Mutual Exclusion

In my implementation, an object obtains exclusive access to shared entities when it executes a check action. Instead of using database concepts, I could employ one of the traditional algorithms for distributed mutual exclusion.

As mentioned in [Ray91], distributed mutual exclusion algorithms are either *permission based* or *token based*. In a token-based approach, the state of a constraint server would be represented as a token that is passed around between the constrained objects. When an object has the token, it has exclusive access to the constraint server represented by the token. If multiple constraint servers constrain the same object, that object would need to access multiple tokens. The need for multiple tokens may lead to deadlock, where two objects wait for each other to pass on a token. Hence, token-based approaches cannot be directly applied to the implementation of synchronizers.

With a permission-based algorithm, an object would obtain exclusive access by asking other objects for permission. In terms of constraint servers, an object would obtain the right to manipulate a server by asking all other objects constrained by the same server. With a permission-based approach, overlapping synchronizers could be handled: if an object is constrained by multiple servers, that object would need to ask any object constrained by either server. Although a permission-based algorithm could handle overlapping synchronizers it would in most cases exhibit a higher message complexity than my algorithm. The message complexity of a permission-based algorithm would be proportional to the number of objects per synchronizer; the message complexity of my algorithm is proportional to the number of synchronizers per object.

It should be observed that certain permission-based algorithms arrange objects in a logical structure such as a tree. By arranging objects in a logical structure, it is possible to reduce the message complexity from a linear function to some sublinear function (e.g., to a logarithmic function) of the number of objects. In our case, because an object needs to communicate with a dynamic number of objects, maintaining such structures would require a lot of bookkeeping. I conclude that a permission-based approach is an improvement only in very special cases; in more typical cases, my algorithm exhibits better message complexity.

5.12   Conclusion

I have described a distributed implementation of synchronizers. The implementation is based on a pessimistic strategy in which constraints are evaluated before messages are dispatched. The implementation is general in that it covers all aspects of synchronizers and synchronization constraints as defined in chapters 2 and 3.

My implementation is an experimental prototype; I have not expended much effort in optimizing it. I believe that a truly optimized implementation requires a compiler for constraints. With a compiler it would be possible to customize the implementation strategy for specific synchronizers.

I have analyzed the implementation both theoretically and empirically. From a theoretical standpoint, I argued that the locking scheme corresponds to two-phase locking for nested transactions. Furthermore, I argued that the implementation is weakly fair: messages that remain legal will eventually be dispatched. The empirical data were obtained from two prototypical applications. I used the dispatch rate as a performance metric to analyze these applications and pointed out some of the fundamental trade-offs involved in implementing constraints.

6 Conclusion

In many distributed systems, correctness requires implementation of message-ordering constraints. It is complicated for the application programmer to implement message-ordering constraints in an ad hoc manner, and it is important that distributed programming languages provide constructs that allow programmers to implement message-ordering constraints in terms of high-level abstractions. We have designed and implemented language constructs that express message-ordering constraints in a high-level and object-oriented manner. In order to maintain object encapsulation and keep object interfaces as abstraction boundaries, I have developed two kinds of language constructs:

- Synchronization constraints describe message-ordering constraints on a per-object basis. These constraints reflect the integrity requirements of a single object, and they are specified as part of that object.

- Synchronizers describe message-ordering constraints for a group of objects. A synchronizer reflects integrity requirements that arise when objects are grouped together. Since a synchronizer is related to an object group rather than individual objects, it is specified as a distinct entity separately from individual objects.

In traditional concurrent languages, the effect of synchronization constraints is described by synchronization mechanisms such as semaphores. With semaphores, synchronization constraints are described as part of the algorithms executed by methods. In contrast, I specify synchronization constraints separately from methods. The philosophy behind this separation is that algorithms and constraints are different design concerns: algorithms specify *how* methods are executed, and constraints specify *when* methods may be executed. The separation of design concerns makes it easier to reason about program correctness, and it supports modularity, which makes it easier to modify and maintain programs.

The separation of synchronization constraints and methods also allows us to integrate synchronization constraints and inheritance. Recently this integration has received much attention. The trend among proposals is to develop increasingly more elaborate, expressive, and flexible notions of synchronization constraints. Recent proposals are also increasingly more complex. As an alternative, I have sought simplicity. The key to simplicity is the assumption that the typical use of inheritance will result in subclass synchronization constraints that are at least as stringent as superclass synchronization constraints. With this assumption, we can design a simple inheritance model in which superclass synchronization constraints are always inherited as is.

Synchronizers describe coordination at the object group level. Few traditional constructs support coordination at the group level. Two exceptions are transactions and atomic multicasts:

- A transaction is a distributed activity that manipulates a group of objects. The semantics of a transaction guarantees that its effect is atomic. If a transaction manipulates (i.e., reads and writes) the state of a group of objects, either all manipulations are executed to completion or no manipulations are executed at all. Moreover, transactions are executed so that they appear to have executed serially, one after the other, in some unspecified order. This consistency notion is called *serializability*. A distributed database is a typical application of transactions. It is essential that each client leaves the database in a consistent state. During a transaction, a client has the illusion of exclusive access to the database even if other clients are concurrently executing their transactions.

- A multicast is a communication that is sent to all objects in a group. When multicasts are atomic, it is guaranteed that two multicast communications are received in the same order at all group members. Replication is a typical application of atomic multicasts. The individual replicas constitute an object group. With replication, it is often essential that all replicas receive communications in the same order.

Transactions and atomic multicasts capture two fundamentally different aspects of distributed coordination: transactions provide consistency in terms of the effect of manipulations, whereas atomic multicasts provide consistency relative to the order in which manipulations occur.

Where atomic multicasts enforce a built-in message order, synchronizers enforce a user-specified message order. Where transactions apply to the effect of activities, synchronizers apply to the relative order of activities. My examples demonstrate that in order to describe distributed systems properly, we need an additional structuring tool to supplement transactions and atomic multicasts. It should be emphasized that I do not intend synchronizers to replace transactions and atomic multicasts. Rather, synchronizers are intended as supplementary tools when building distributed systems.

In traditional distributed languages, user-defined message-ordering constraints for a group of objects can be implemented only by modifying the objects to coordinate their actions explicitly through the exchange of control communication. Such control protocols are complicated to develop, cannot be composed, and cannot be defined and enforced in a manner that is transparent to the involved objects.

The transparency provided by synchronizers is essential for building distributed applications by gluing together reusable asynchronous objects. My examples show that gluing together asynchronous objects into an object group often gives rise to message-ordering constraints for the group. In order to reuse the objects, it must be possible to enforce the group-level message-ordering constraints transparently, that is, without changing the objects.

It is a challenge to develop an efficient implementation of message-ordering constraints. Since the ordering constraints are described in terms of Boolean conditions, an important goal for the implementation is to minimize the number of times that a condition is (re)tested. In order to address this goal, it is necessary to determine the relationships between methods and conditions, that is, which methods influence which conditions. To determine this relationship, we need static analysis techniques and thereby compiler support. Static analysis of constraints is an important topic for future work.

With synchronizers, multiple objects may concurrently attempt to test the same condition in a common synchronizer and collide since they cannot both gain exclusive access to the synchronizer. It is critical for the performance of synchronizers to avoid these collisions. I have found that the number of collisions is highly dependent on the heuristics used for notifying objects about state changes at a synchronizer. The dependence between collisions and notifications is present because a notification message from a synchronizer causes an object to recheck the constraints at that synchronizer. I have experimented with different notification heuristics and have found a trade-off between the level of concurrency and the number of collisions. We can avoid collisions by notifying objects one at a time, which essentially eliminates concurrency; or we can create "maximal" concurrency by notifying all objects at the same time, which potentially leads to collisions. Making an efficient trade-off requires static analysis techniques so that a synchronizer knows which objects are actually affected by a state change. This would allow synchronizers to be more selective in their notification scheme.

Although performance is an important metric for a language construct, the ease with which a construct enables programmers to build and reason about a distributed application is as important. Ultimately an evaluation of constructs would require empirical studies of programmer productivity with and without support for synchronizers and synchronization constraints. Such empirical studies are beyond the scope of my current work.

My efforts have concentrated on the essence of synchronizers and synchronization constraints. I have strived for simplicity and orthogonality in developing the constructs. My goal has been to capture the fundamental principles that should be supported, hoping to influence the design of future distributed languages. In focusing on fundamental principles, I have deliberately ignored a number of issues that would increase the expressiveness of my constructs:

- *Communication with synchronizers.* I have insisted that synchronizers cannot receive messages directly; they can only observe message dispatch by objects. In certain situations it may be awkward to affect the behavior of synchronizers indirectly through their observation of messages. It may be more elegant simply to send a message directly to synchronizers.

- *User-defined events.* The constraints and triggers in a synchronizer are concerned only with events that denote the dispatch of a message. In some cases, it is desirable to observe other events, such as the completion of method executions. The ability to define constraints and triggers over user-defined events would make constructs more expressive.

- *Scoped pattern matching.* The binding between synchronizers and messages is based on pattern matching. There are situations that would benefit from the binding of synchronizers to specific messages sent within a given block of code. It is possible, although tedious, to express this kind of binding using pattern matching: the programmer could explicitly tag all messages sent within a given block of code and construct patterns that match only the tagged messages. However, from a programming standpoint, tagging is not an elegant way to express this.

- *Set-based patterns*. My patterns are designed so that each one matches messages only for one method. In many situations, the same constraints apply to multiple methods. This calls for patterns that can apply to multiple rather than single methods.

There is more to supporting a given style of programming than merely providing a set of language abstractions. It is necessary to provide a set of tools that help programmers construct, execute, and analyze programs. Using synchronizers and synchronization constraints for the construction of distributed systems will require tools that support these constructs. Building a complete programming environment to support developing applications using synchronizers and synchronization constraints is another important direction for future work.

Glossary

actor A semantic entity that represents a concurrent object.

asynchronous message passing Sending a message is a nonblocking operation: the sender of a message does not wait for the message to reach its destination.

atomicity constraint An atomicity constraint is specified in a synchronizer. It prevents certain messages from being dispatched individually, and it enables certain message sets to be dispatched as an indivisible action.

check action A distributed activity that evaluates the constraints for a given message and, if the constraints are satisfied, dispatches the message and evaluates its triggers.

class A template for objects. Objects are created by instantiating a class. Objects created from the same class have the same structure but individual states.

configuration A mathematical entity that represents a snapshot of a distributed system in the semantics.

constraint A common term for atomicity constraints and disabling constraints.

constraint evaluation The act of determining whether a specific constraint delays the dispatch of a specific message or message set.

constraint function A mathematical construct used to represent constraints in the semantics. Application of constraint functions represents constraint evaluation.

constraint satisfaction A message or a message set satisfies a constraint if the constraint does not delay its dispatch.

constraint server An implementation level entity that represents a synchronizer.

disabling constraint A disabling constraint is specified in a synchronizer. A disabling constraint defines a Boolean condition for message dispatch.

dispatch The activity performed by an object when it starts to execute one of its methods in response to a message.

dispatch rate The percentage of check actions that result in message dispatch.

event diagram A pictorial representation of a collection of objects and the messages they exchange during some time interval.

fairness A requirement that messages are eventually dispatched.

inheritance An asymmetric relationship between two classes. Allows a class, called a subclass, to be defined as a refinement of another class, called a superclass.

initiating object An object that initiates a check action.

input queue A per-object data structure in which objects store incoming messages until they can be dispatched.

leaf message A message that is included in a check action.

message An entity used for interobject communication. A message has a unique sender object and a unique receiver object and represents a request made by the sender to invoke a method in the receiver.

message-ordering constraint A requirement that messages are dispatched in a specific order. A message-ordering constraint is dictated by the integrity of individual objects or by the integrity of object groups. I specify message-ordering constraints in the form of synchronization constraints and synchronizers.

method A procedure defined as part of an object. A method may be part of an object's interface, in which case other objects may request invocation of the method by means of message passing.

method table A per-object data structure that contains information about the disabling constraints, atomicity constraints, and triggers enforced on the object.

object A software entity with its own state and a number of procedures to manipulate this state. The state of an object is encapsulated by an interface that constitutes an abstraction boundary between the object and its environment. Objects have their own thread of control.

participating object An object that participates in a check action.

pattern An abstraction that identifies a collection of messages—the messages that match the pattern. A pattern identifies messages that are all destined for the same method in the same object.

root message The starting point of a check action.

subclass A class defined as a refinement of another class by means of inheritance.

superclass A class used to define other classes by means of refinement under inheritance.

synchronization constraints A per-object specification of message-ordering constraints.

synchronizer A per-object group specification of message-ordering constraints.

transition relation A relation between configurations. For a given configuration, a transition relation determines the future configurations that are possible after one execution step.

trigger A trigger is specified in a synchronizer. A trigger executes an action when certain messages are dispatched by a specified object. The actions executed by a trigger may update the state of the enclosing synchronizer.

trigger evaluation The act of executing the trigger actions caused by the dispatch of a specific message.

References

[AFK+93]   G. Agha, S. Frølund, W. Kim, R. Panwar, A. Patterson, and D. C. Sturman. Abstraction and Modularity Mechanisms for Concurrent Computing. *IEEE Parallel & Distributed Technology, Systems and Applications*, 1(2), May 1993.

[AFL90]   P. C. Attie, I. R. Forman, and E. Levy. On Fairness as an Abstraction for the Design of Distributed Systems. In *Proceedings of the Tenth International Conference on Distributed Computing Systems*. IEEE, 1990.

[Agh86]   G. Agha. *Actors: A Model of Concurrent Computation in Distributed Systems*. MIT Press, 1986.

[AGMB91]   C. Atkinson, S. Goldsack, A. D. Maio, and R. Bayan. Object-Oriented Concurrency and Distribution in DRAGOON. *Journal of Object-Oriented Programming*, 4(1), March/April 1991.

[AKP94]   G. Agha, W. Kim, and R. Panwar. Actor Languages for Specification of Parallel Computations. In G. E. Blelloch, K. Mani Chandy, and S. Jagannathan, editors, *DIMACS. Series in Discrete Mathematics and Theoretical Computer Science. Vol. 18. Specification of Parallel Algorithms*, pages 239–258. American Mathematical Society, 1994. Proceedings of DIMACS '94 Workshop.

[Ame87]   P. America. POOL-T: A Parallel Object-Oriented Language. In A. Yonezawa and M. Tokoro, editors, *Object-Oriented Concurrent Programming*, pages 199–220. MIT Press, 1987.

[Ame90]   P. America. A Parallel Object-Oriented Language with Inheritance and Subtyping. In *Proceedings OOPSLA/ECOOP '90*, pages 161–168, October 1990. Published as ACM SIGPLAN Notices, volume 25, number 10.

[AMST92]   G. Agha, I. A. Mason, S. Smith, and C. L. Talcott. Towards a Theory of Actor Computation. In *Proceedings of the Third International Conference on Concurrency Theory (CONCUR '92)*, LNCS 630, pages 565–579. Springer-Verlag, August 1992.

[AMST96]   G. Agha, I. A. Mason, S. Smith, and C. L. Talcott. A Foundation for Actor Computation. *Journal of Functional Programming*, 1996. (To appear).

[And91]   G. R. Andrews. *Concurrent Programming: Principles and Practice*. The Benjamin/Cummings Publishing Company, 1991.

[And92a]   B. Andersen. Ellie: A General, Fine-Grained, First-Class, Object-Based Language. *Journal of Object-Oriented Programming*, 5(2), May 1992.

[And92b]   B. Andersen. Fine-Grained Parallelism in Ellie. *Journal of Object-Oriented Programming*, 5(3), June 1992.

[AOC+88]   G. R. Andrews, R. A. Olsson, M. Coffin, I. Elshoff, K. Nielsen, T. Purdin, and G. Townsend. An Overview of the SR Language and Implementation. *ACM Transactions on Programming Languages and Systems*, 10(1), January 1988.

[Ara91]   C. Arapis. Temporal Specifications of Object Behavior. In B. Thalheim, J. Demetrovics, and H.-D. Gerhardt, editors, *Third Symposium on Mathematical Fundamentals of Database and Knowledge Base Systems*, LNCS 495, pages 308–324. Springer-Verlag, 1991.

[Ast91]   E. Astesiano.   Inductive and Operational Semantics.   In E. J.
             Neuhold and M. Paul, editors, *Formal Description of Programming
             Concepts—IFIP State of the Art Reports*. Springer-Verlag, 1991.

[AWY93]   G. Agha, P. Wegner, and A. Yonezawa, editors. *Research Directions
             in Concurrent Object-Oriented Programming*. MIT Press, 1993.

[Bar84]   H. P. Barendegt. *The Lambda Calculus—Its Syntax and Semantics*,
             volume 103 of *Studies in Logic*. Elsevier Science Publishers B. V.,
             revised edition, 1984.

[BBV78]   Y. Bekker, J. Briat, and J. P. Verjus. Construction of a Synchro-
             nization Scheme by Independent Definition of Parallelism. In P. G.
             Hibbard and S. A. Schuman, editors, *Constructing Quality Software*.
             North-Holland Publishing Company, 1978.

[BHL91]   G. Blakowski, J. Hübel, and U. Langrehr. Tools for Specifying and
             Executing Synchronized Multimedia Presentations. In *Proceedings
             of the Second International Workshop on Network and Operating
             System Support for Digital Audio and Video*, LNCS 614. Springer-
             Verlag, 1991.

[BJ87]   K. P. Birman and T. A. Joseph. Reliable Communication in the
             Presence of Failures. *ACM Transactions on Computer Systems*, 5(1),
             February 1987.

[BKS88]   R. J. R. Back and R. Kurki-Suonio. Distributed Cooperation with
             Action Systems. *ACM Transactions on Programming Languages and
             Systems*, 10(4), 1988.

[Bro93]   L. Brown, editor. *The New Shorter Oxford English Dictionary*. Ox-
             ford University Press, 1993.

[BSY92]   P. A. Buhr, R. A. Strooboscher, and B. M. Younger. μ-C++: Con-
             currency in the Object-Oriented Language C++. *Software—Practice
             and Experience*, 22(2), February 1992.

[Car84]   L. Cardelli. A Semantics of Multiple Inheritance. In *Semantics of
             Data Types*. Springer-Verlag, 1984.

[Car90]   D. Caromel. Concurrency and Reusability: From Sequential to Paral-
             lel. *Journal of Object-Oriented Programming*, 3(3), September 1990.

[CH74]   R. H. Campbell and A. N. Habermann. The Specification Of Process
             Synchronisation by Path Expressions. In E. Gelenbe and C. Kaiser,
             editors, *International Symposium on Operating Systems*, LNCS 16.
             Springer Verlag, 1974.

[Cha87]   A. Charlesworth. The Multiway Rendezvous. *ACM Transactions on
             Programming Languages and Systems*, 9(2), July 1987.

[CNY95]   P. Ciancarini, O. Nierstrasz, and A. Yonezawa, editors. *Object-Based
             Models and Languages for Concurrent Systems*. LNCS 924. Springer-
             Verlag, 1995.

[Con63]   M. E. Conway. Design of a Separable Transition-Diagram Compiler.
             Communications of the ACM, 6(7), July 1963.

[Coo89]   W. Cook. *A Denotational Semantics of Inheritance*. Ph.D. thesis,
             Brown University, 1989.

[CR82]   O. Carvalho and G. Roucairol. On the Distribution of an Assertion.
             In *Proceedings of the First Conference on Principles of Distributed
             Computing*, pages 121–131. ACM, 1982.

[CW84]   L. Cardelli and P. Wegner. On Understanding Types, Data Abstraction, and Polymorphism. *ACM Computing Surveys*, 17(4), Dec 1984.

[DDR+91]   D. Decouchant, P. Le Dot, M. Riveill, C. Roisin, and X. Rousset de Pina. A Synchronization Mechanism for an Object Oriented Distributed System. In *Proceedings of the Eleventh International Conference on Distributed Computing Systems*. IEEE, 1991.

[DHW88]   D. L. Detlefs, M. P. Herlihy, and J. M. Wing. Inheritance of Synchronization and Recovery Properties in Avalon/C++. *IEEE Computer*, 21(12):57–69, December 1988.

[Dij68]   E. W. Dijkstra. Cooperating Sequential Processes. In F. Genuys, editor, *Programming Languages*. Academic Press, 1968.

[DMN68]   O.-J. Dahl, B. Myhrhaug, and K. Nygaard. Simula 67 Common Base Language. Technical Report Publication S-2, Norwegian Computing Center, 1968.

[EFK89]   M. Evangelist, N. Francez, and S. Katz. Multiparty Interactions for Interprocess Communication and Synchronization. *IEEE Transactions on Software Engineering*, 15(11), 1989.

[ESFG88]   M. Evangelist, V. Y. Shen, I. R. Forman, and M. Graf. Using Raddle to Design Distributed Systems. In *Proceedings of the Tenth International Conference on Software Engineering*. IEEE, 1988.

[FA93]   S. Frølund and G. Agha. A Language Framework for Multi-Object Coordination. In O. Nierstrasz, editor, *Proceedings of ECOOP '93*, LNCS 707. Springer-Verlag, 1993.

[FA95]   S. Frølund and G. Agha. Abstracting Interactions Based on Message Sets. In P. Ciancarini, O. Nierstrasz, and A. Yonezawa, editors, *Object-Based Models and Languages for Concurrent Systems*, LNCS 924. Springer-Verlag, 1995.

[FBB92]   B. N. Freeman-Benson and A. Borning. Integrating Constraints with an Object-Oriented Language. In O. Lehrmann Madsen, editor, *Proceedings ECOOP '92*, LNCS 615, pages 268–286. Springer-Verlag, July 1992.

[Fel87]   M. Felleisen. *The Calculi of Lambda-ν-CS Conversion: A Syntactic Theory of Control and State in Imperative Higher-Order Programming Languages*. Ph.D. thesis, Indiana University, August 1987.

[FF84]   R. E. Filman and D. P. Friedman. *Coordinated Computing*. McGraw-Hill, 1984.

[FHT86]   N. Francez, B. Hailpern, and G. Taubenfeld. Script: A Communication Abstraction Mechanism and Its Verification. *Science of Computer Programming*, 6:35–88, 1986.

[Fra86]   N. Francez. *Fairness*. Texts and Monographs in Computer Science. Springer-Verlag, 1986.

[Frø92]   S. Frølund. Inheritance of Synchronization Constraints in Concurrent Object-Oriented Programming Languages. In O. Lehrmann Madsen, editor, *Proceedings ECOOP '92*, LNCS 615, pages 185–196. Springer-Verlag, July 1992.

[GC86]   J. E. Grass and R. H. Campbell. Mediators: A Synchronization Mechanism. In *Sixth International Conference on Distributed Computing Systems*. IEEE, 1986.

[GCLR92] R. Guerraoui, R. Capobianchi, A. Lanusse, and P. Roux. Nesting Actions through Asynchronous Message Passing: The ACS Protocol. In O. Lehrmann Madsen, editor, *Proceedings ECOOP '92*, LNCS 615, pages 170–184. Springer-Verlag, July 1992.

[Gib91] S. Gibbs. Composite Multimedia and Active Objects. In *Proceedings OOPSLA '91*, pages 97–112, November 1991. Published as ACM SIGPLAN Notices, volume 26, number 11.

[Han75] P. B. Hansen. The Programming Language Concurrent Pascal. *IEEE Transactions on Software Engineering*, 1(2), June 1975.

[Har86] D. M. Harland. *Concurrency and Programming Languages*. John Wiley and Sons, 1986.

[Hen90] M. Hennessy. *The Semantics of Programming Languages*. John Wiley and Sons, 1990.

[Hew77] C. Hewitt. Viewing Control Structures as Patterns of Passing Messages. *Journal of Artificial Intelligence*, 8(3):323–364, 1977.

[HHG90] R. Helm, I. M. Holland, and D. Gangopadhyay. Contracts: Specifying Behavioural Compositions in Object-Oriented Systems. In *Proceedings OOPSLA/ECOOP '90*, pages 169–180, October 1990. Published as ACM SIGPLAN Notices, volume 25, number 10.

[HJ90] J. Hearne and D. Jusak. The Tahiti Programming Language: Events as First-Class Objects. In *Proceedings of the Third International Conference on Computer Languages*. IEEE, 1990.

[Hoa74] C. A. R. Hoare. Monitors: An Operating System Structuring Concept. *Communications of the ACM*, 17(10), October 1974.

[Hoa78] C. A. R. Hoare. Communicating Sequential Processes. *Communications of the ACM*, 21(8):666–677, August 1978.

[Hol92] I. M. Holland. Specifying Reusable Components Using Contracts. In O. Lehrmann Madsen, editor, *Proceedings ECOOP '92*, LNCS 615, pages 287–308. Springer-Verlag, July 1992.

[Ish92] Y. Ishikawa. Communication Mechanism on Autonomous Objects. In *Proceedings OOPSLA '92*, pages 303–314, October 1992. Published as ACM SIGPLAN Notices, volume 27, number 10.

[Isl95] N. Islam. *Distributed Objects; Methodologies for Customizing Operating Systems*. IEEE Computer Society Press, 1995.

[JS91] Y. Joung and S. A. Smolka. Coordinating First-Order Multiparty Interactions. In *Proceedings of the Eighteenth Conference on Principles of Programming Languages*. ACM, 1991.

[Kah88] G. Kahn. Natural Semantics. In K. Fuchi and M. Nivat, editors, *Programming Future Generation Computers*. North-Holland Publishing Company, 1988.

[KHPW90] G. E. Kaiser, W. Hseush, S. S. Popovich, and S. F. Wu. Multiple Concurrency Control Policies in an Object-Oriented Programming System. In *Proceedings of the Second Symposium on Parallel and Distributed Processing*. IEEE, December 1990.

[KL89] D. G. Kafura and K. Hae Lee. Inheritance in Actor Based Concurrent Object-Oriented Languages. In S. Cook, editor, *Proceedings ECOOP '89*, pages 131–145. Cambridge University Press, July 1989.

[KLG93]   S. Kaplan, J. P. Loyall, and S. K. Goering.   Specifying Concur-
            rent Languages and Systems with Δ-GRAMMARS. In G. Agha,
            P. Wegner, and A. Yonezawa, editors, *Research Directions in Object-
            Oriented Programming*. MIT Press, 1993.

[KWN90]   D. G. Kafura, D. Washabaugh, and J. Nelson. Garbage Collection
            of Actors. In *Proceedings OOPSLA/ECOOP '90*, pages 126–134,
            October 1990. Published as ACM SIGPLAN Notices, volume 25,
            number 10.

[Lan64]   P. J. Landin. The Mechanical Evaluation of Expressions. *The Com-
            puter Journal*, 6(4):308–320, January 1964.

[Lel88]   W. Leler. *Constraint Programming Languages—Their Specification
            and Generation*. Addison-Wesley, 1988.

[LR80]   B. W. Lampson and D. D. Redell. Experience with Processes and
            Monitors in Mesa. *Communications of the ACM*, 23(2), February
            1980.

[LS82]   B. Liskov and R. Scheifler. Guardians and Actions: Linguistic Sup-
            port for Robust, Distributed Programs. In *Proceedings of the Ninth
            Symposium on Principles of Programming Languages*, pages 7–19.
            ACM, January 1982.

[McH94]   C. McHale. *Synchronisation in Concurrent, Object-oriented Lan-
            guages: Expressive Power, Genericity and Inheritance*. Ph.D. thesis,
            Department of Computer Science, Trinity College, Dublin, October
            1994.

[Mes93a]   J. Meseguer. A Logical Theory of Concurrent Objects and Its Re-
            alization in the Maude Language. In G. Agha, P. Wegner, and
            A. Yonezawa, editors, *Research Directions in Concurrent Object-
            Oriented Programming*. MIT Press, 1993.

[Mes93b]   J. Meseguer. Solving the Inheritance Anomaly in Concurrent Object-
            Oriented programming. In O. Nierstrasz, editor, *Proceedings of
            ECOOP '93*, LNCS 707. Springer-Verlag, 1993.

[Mey85]   B. Meyer. *Object-oriented Software Construction*. Prentice-Hall,
            1985.

[Mos85]   J. E. B. Moss. *Nested Transactions: An Approach to Reliable Dis-
            tributed Computing*. MIT Press, 1985.

[MPN93]   O. L. Madsen, B. M. Pedersen, and K. Nygaard. *Object-Oriented
            Programming in the BETA Programming Language*. Addison-Wesley,
            June 1993.

[MPS91]   S. Mishra, L. L. Peterson, and R. D. Schlichting. Consul: A Commu-
            nication Substrate for Fault-Tolerant Distributed Programs. Techni-
            cal report, University of Arizona, Tucson, 1991.

[MT91]   I. A. Mason and C. L. Talcott. Equivalence in Functional Languages
            with Effect. *Journal of Functional Programming*, 1:287–327, 1991.

[MTY93]   S. Matsuoka, K. Taura, and A. Yonezawa. Highly Efficient and En-
            capsulated Re-use of Synchronization Code in Concurrent Object-
            Oriented Languages. In *Proceedings OOPSLA '93*, pages 109–126,
            October 1993. Published as ACM SIGPLAN Notices, volume 28,
            number 10.

[Mul89]   S. Mullender, editor. *Distributed Systems*. Addison-Wesley, 1989.

[MWBD91]   C. McHale, B. Walsh, S. Baker, and A. Donnelly. Scheduling Predicates. In M. Tokoro, O. Nierstrasz, and P. Wegner, editors, *Object-Based Concurrent Computing*, LNCS 612, pages 177–193. Springer-Verlag, July 1991.

[MY93]   S. Matsuoka and A. Yonezawa. Analysis of Inheritance Anomaly in Object-Oriented Concurrent Programming Languages. In G. Agha, P. Wegner, and A. Yonezawa, editors, *Research Directions in Object-Oriented Programming*. MIT Press, 1993.

[Neu91]   C. Neusius. Synchronizing Actions. In P. America, editor, *Proceedings ECOOP '91*, LNCS 512, pages 118–132. Springer-Verlag, July 1991.

[Nie87]   O. Nierstrasz. Active Objects in Hybrid. In *Proceedings OOPSLA '87*, pages 243–253, December 1987. Published as ACM SIGPLAN Notices, volume 22, number 12.

[OOW91]   M. H. Olsen, E. Oskiewicz, and J. P. Warne. A Model for Interface Groups. In *Proceedings of the Tenth Symposium on Reliable Distributed Systems*. IEEE, 1991.

[Pan96]   R. B. Panwar. *Specification of Resource Management Strategies for Concurrent Objects*. Ph.D. thesis, University of Illinois at Urbana-Champaign, 1996.

[Pap92]   M. Papathomas. *Language Design Rationale and Semantic Framework for Concurrent Object-Oriented Programming*. Ph.D. thesis, University of Geneva, January 1992. Published as Technical Report, Thesis Number 2522.

[PBGdM93]   M. Papathomas, C. Breiteneder, S. Gibbs, and V. de Mey. Synchronization in Virtual Worlds. In N. Magnenat and D. Thalmann, editors, *Virtual Worlds and Multimedia*. John Wiley and Sons, 1993.

[Pet77]   J. L. Peterson. Petri Nets. *ACM Computing Surveys*, 9(3), September 1977.

[PS94]   J. Palsberg and M. I. Schwartzbach. *Object-Oriented Type Systems*. John Wiley and Sons, 1994.

[PV83]   Y. Parker and J. P. Verjus, editors. *Distributed Computing Systems*. Academic Press, 1983.

[Ray88]   M. Raynal. *Networks and Distributed Computation*. The MIT Press, 1988.

[Ray91]   M. Raynal. A Simple Taxonomy for Distributed Mutual Exclusion Algorithms. *ACM Operating Systems Review*, pages 47–49, 1991.

[Rep92]   J. H. Reppy. *Higher-Order Concurrency*. Ph.D. thesis, Cornell University, June 1992. Published as Technical Report 92-1285.

[Riv95]   M. Riveill. Synchronising Shared Objects. *Distributed Systems Engineering Journal*, pages 1–14, June 1995.

[RSI78]   D. J. Rosenkrantz, R. E. Stearns, and P. M. Lewis II. System Level Concurrency Control for Distributed Database Systems. *ACM Transactions on Database Systems*, 3(2):178–198, June 1978.

[RTL+91]   R. K. Raj, E. Tempero, H. M. Levy, A. P. Black, N. C. Hutchinson, and E. Jul. Emerald: A General-Purpose Programming Language. *Software—Practice and Experience*, 21(1), January 1991.

[SA94]   D. C. Sturman and G. Agha. A Protocol Description Language for
             Customizing Failure Semantics. In *Proceedings of the Thirteenth
             Symposium on Reliable Distributed Systems*, pages 148–157. IEEE,
             October 1994.

[Shi91]   E. Shibayama.   Reuse of Concurrent Object Descriptions.   In
             A. Yonezawa and T. Ito, editors, *Concurrency: Theory, Language,
             and Architecture*, LNCS 491. Springer-Verlag, 1991.

[SPG91]   A. Silberschatz, J. Peterson, and P. Galvin. *Operating Systems Con-
             cepts*. Addison-Wesley, third edition, 1991.

[Ste80]   G. L. Steele. The Definition and Implementation of a Computer Pro-
             gramming Language Based on Constraints. Technical Report AI-TR-
             595, MIT, 1980.

[Ste90]   R. Steinmetz. Synchronization Properties in Multimedia Systems.
             IEEE Journal on Selected Areas in Communications, 8:401–412,
             April 1990.

[Stu94]   D. C. Sturman.   Fault-Adaptation for Systems in Unpredictable
             Environments.   Master's thesis, University of Illinois at Urbana-
             Champaign, January 1994.

[TA88]   A. Tripathi and M. Aksit. Communication, Scheduling, and Resource
             Management in SINA.   *Journal of Object Oriented Programming*,
             1(4):24–37, November 1988.

[Tho87]   K. S. Thomsen. Inheritance on Processes, Exemplified on Distributed
             Termination Detection. *International Journal of Parallel Program-
             ming*, 16(1), February 1987.

[TS89]   C. Tomlinson and V. Singh. Inheritance and Synchronization with
             Enabled Sets. In *Proceedings OOPSLA '89*, pages 103–112, October
             1989. Published as ACM SIGPLAN Notices, volume 24, number 10.

[Uni82]   United States Department of Defense. *Reference Manual for the Ada
             Language*, draft, revised mil-std 1815 edition, July 1982.

[VAT92]   N. Venkatasubramanian, G. Agha, and C. L. Talcott. Scalable Dis-
             tributed Garbage Collection for Systems of Active Objects. In *Pro-
             ceedings of the International Workshop on Memory Management*,
             LNCS 637, 1992.

[vdBL91]   J. van den Bos and C. Laffra.   PROCOL, a Concurrent Object-
             Oriented Language with Protocols Delegation and Constraints. *Acta
             Informatica*, 28:511–538, 1991.

[Vis88]   P. Vishnubhotla. Synchronization and Scheduling in ALPS Objects.
             In *Proceedings of the Eighth International Conference on Distributed
             Computing Systems*. IEEE, 1988.

[WF91]   A. Wright and M. Felleisen. A Syntactic Approach to Type Sound-
             ness. Technical Report COMP TR91-160, Rice University, April 1991.

[Win89]   G. Winskel. An Introduction to Event Structures. In J. W. de Bakker,
             W.-P. de Roever, and G. Rozenberg, editors, *Linear Time, Branch-
             ing Time and Partial Order in Logics and Models for Concurrency*,
             LNCS 354. Springer-Verlag, 1989.

[WL88]   C. T. Wilkes and R. J. LeBlanc. Distributed Locking: A Mechanism
             for Constructing Highly Available Objects. In *Proceedings of the
             Seventh Symposium on Reliable Distributed Systems*. IEEE, 1988.

[WY91]   K. Wakita and A. Yonezawa. Linguistic Supports for Development of
            Distributed Organizational Information Systems in Object-Oriented
            Concurrent Computation Frameworks. In *Proceedings of the First
            Conference on Organizational Computing Systems*. ACM, September
            1991.

[WZ88]   P. Wegner and S. B. Zdonik. Inheritance as an Incremental Modi-
            fication Mechanism or What Like Is and Isn't Like. In S. Gjessing
            and K. Nygaard, editors, *Proceedings ECOOP '88*, LNCS 322, pages
            55–77. Springer-Verlag, August 1988.

[Yon90]   A. Yonezawa, editor. *ABCL: An Object-Oriented Concurrent Sys-
            tem*. MIT Press, 1990.

Name Index

Subject Index